What A World 3

Amazing Stories from Around the Globe

Milada Broukal

Longman

What A World 3: Amazing Stories from Around the Globe

Pearson Education, 10 Bank Street, White Plains, NY 10606

Executive editor: Laura Le Dréan
Acquisitions editor: Lucille M. Kennedy
Development editors: Mykan White, Andrea Bryant
Senior production editor: Robert Ruvo
Vice president, marketing: Kate McLoughlin
Marketing manager: Timothy Benell
Senior manufacturing buyer: Nancy Flaggman
Photo research: Dana Klinek
Cover design: Elizabeth Carlson
Text composition: NK Graphics
Text font: 12/15 New Aster

Photo credits:
  page 1, © Stapleton Collection/Corbis; **page 11,** © Danny Lehman/Corbis;
  page 22, © Aman Sharma/Associated Press; **page 32,** © Bettmann/Corbis;
  page 42, © Bettmann/Corbis; **page 52,** © Hulton Archive/Getty Images;
  page 62, © Macduff Everton/Corbis; **page 72,** © Ariel Skelley/Corbis;
  page 86, © Mary Altaffer/Associated Press; **page 97,** © S.P. Gillette/Corbis;
  page 108, © Alinari Archives/Corbis; **page 119,** © Tom Miletic/Associated
  Press; **page 130,** © Catherine Karnow/Corbis; **page 141,** © Craig
  Lovell/Corbis; **page152,** © Christie's Images/Corbis; **page 163,** © Elisc
  Amendola/Associated Press.

What A World **reviewers:**
Nanette Dougherty, Jackson Heights School, Jackson Heights, NY; **Denise
Selleck,** City College of San Francisco, San Francisco, CA; **Anthony
Halderman,** Cuesta College, San Luis Obispo, CA; **Julie Gunzelman Un,**
Massasoit Community College, Brockton, MA

Library of Congress Cataloging-in-Publication Data
Broukal, Milada.
   What a world 3 : amazing stories from around the globe / Milada Broukal.
      p. cm.
   Includes index.
   ISBN 0-13-048465-2
   1. English language—Textbooks for foreign speakers. 2. Readers—Manners
and customs. I. Title. II. Title: What a world three.
   PE1128.B71663   2005
   428.6'4—dc22   2005002976

ISBN: 0-13-048465-2

Printed in the United States of America
6 7 8 9 10–VHJ–09

CONTENTS

INTRODUCTION   v

Unit 1   What Is the Legend of King Arthur?   1
Unit 2   Why Did the Inca Empire Disappear?   11
Unit 3   How Do Hindus Celebrate the Diwali Festival?   22
Unit 4   What Is the Story Behind *The 1,001 Arabian Nights*?   32
Unit 5   Who Were the Samurai?   42
Unit 6   What Does Hair Tell Us About People?   52
Unit 7   How Did Chopsticks Originate?   62
Unit 8   Where Did Certain Wedding Customs Come From?   72
Self-Test 1   Units 1–8   82
Unit 9   Who Are the CyberAngels?   86
Unit 10   Why Do People Want to Climb Mount Everest?   97
Unit 11   Why Is the Renaissance Important?   108
Unit 12   What Is the Most Popular Sport in the World?   119
Unit 13   How Did Convicts Help Settle Australia?   130
Unit 14   How Do Greetings Differ Around the World?   141
Unit 15   Why Is Napoleon Famous?   152
Unit 16   Who Invented the World Wide Web?   163
Self-Test 2   Units 9–16   174

APPENDICES
  Word List   179
  Map of the World   182
  Index to the Grammar and Punctuation Activities   184

INTRODUCTION

What A World 3: Amazing Stories from Around the Globe is an intermediate reader. It is the third in a three-book series of readings for English language learners. Sixteen topics have been selected for this book. Each topic is about a different person, place, or custom. The topics span history and the globe, from the Samurai, to the celebration of the Diwali festival, to the invention of the World Wide Web.

Every unit begins with a question and answers that question. Each unit contains:

- A prereading activity
- A reading passage (900–1200 words)
- Topic-related vocabulary work
- Comprehension exercises, including pair work
- Discussion questions
- A writing activity
- A grammar and punctuation activity

BEFORE YOU READ opens with a picture of the person, place, or custom featured in the unit. Prereading questions follow. Their purpose is to motivate students to read, encourage predictions about the content of the reading, and involve the students' own experiences when possible. Vocabulary can be presented as the need arises.

The **READING** passage should be first done individually by skimming for the general content. The teacher may wish to explain the bolded vocabulary words at this point. The students should then do a second, closer reading. Further reading(s) can be done aloud.

The two **VOCABULARY** exercises focus on the bold words in the reading. *Meaning*, a definition exercise, encourages students to work out the meanings from the context. Within this group are *Words That Go Together* which are collocations or groups of words which are easier to learn together the way they are used in the language. The second exercise, *Use*, reinforces the vocabulary further by making students use the words in a meaningful, yet possibly different, context. This section can be done during or after the reading phase, or both.

There are several **COMPREHENSION** exercises. Each unit contains *Understanding Main Ideas*, *Remembering Details*, and *Making Inferences*. All confirm the content of the text either in general or in detail. These exercises for developing reading skills can be done individually, in pairs, in small groups, or as a class. It is preferable to do these exercises in conjunction with the text, since they are not meant to test memory.

DISCUSSION questions encourage students to bring their own ideas and imagination to the related topics in each reading. They can also provide insights into cultural similarities and differences.

WRITING provides the stimulus for students to write a paragraph or an essay about the reading. Teachers should use their own discretion when deciding whether or not to correct the writing exercises.

GRAMMAR AND PUNCTUATION provides basic rules and accompanying activities for grammar or punctuation, using examples from the readings. An index listing the Grammar and Punctuation activities can be found on page 184.

SELF-TESTS after Unit 8 and Unit 16 review sentence structure, vocabulary, and grammar and punctuation in a multiple-choice format.

If you would like the Answer Key for *What A World 3*, please contact Pearson Longman.
Customers in the United States: ESLSampling@pearsoned.com
Customers outside the United States: elt@pearsoned.com

UNIT 1

What Is the Legend of King Arthur?

BEFORE YOU READ

Answer these questions.

1. What is a legend?
2. What famous legends do you know?
3. What are some movies which are based on legends? Why are they popular?

What Is the Legend of King Arthur?

1 The legend of King Arthur and the Knights of the Round Table makes us think of an age of heroism and romance. For a thousand years, stories about them have been **passed down from** generation to generation, across Europe and the rest of the world. We even **encounter** them today in books, on television, and in the movies. In all these stories, King Arthur and his knights fight bravely for justice and truth. Of course, they always win.

2 The legendary King Arthur was **known as** the greatest king that ever lived. His magnificent castle was called Camelot, and his wife, Guinevere, was the most beautiful woman in history. Arthur had the greatest knights at his court. They were all equal and sat at a round table to show that no one had a higher rank than the other. The most famous knights were Sir Gawain and Sir Lancelot. The knights did many **good deeds** and went on adventures. They saved young women **in trouble** and searched for a **precious** cup called the Holy Grail. They were all heroes, although they had faults like all people do.

3 In the legend, Arthur is the perfect king. He has a wizard by the name of Merlin who helps him defeat his enemies. He also has flashing swords and wears a fine suit of shining armor. Arthur has two magic swords. At the beginning of his reign, he pulls one from a block of stone, proving that he is the true king. The other sword appears in the middle of a lake and has powers that make Arthur immortal. At the end of his reign, Arthur returns to the lake and disappears into the **mist.**

4 Are these stories true? Did King Arthur really exist? Was his wife, Guinevere, real? Did Camelot exist? How true to fact are some of these stories? Historians don't know. For the last few hundred years, people thought that the legend about Arthur had been invented. However, historians have realized recently that Arthur really may have existed. Most historians believe that he probably did. They think that he was a king or a great leader somewhere in Great Britain. Most believe that Arthur lived around the end of the fifth and beginning of the sixth century. They also believe that he led an army against the Saxons who invaded Britain a very long time ago, that he won this great battle, and that he was the character who **inspired** hundreds of stories.

5 The stories about Arthur may have some truths in them, but they also have a lot of exaggerations. It seems difficult to separate fact from fiction. Some people question how a man could win so many battles and sword fights without getting wounded or killed. And some of the things that Arthur's adviser Merlin says and does are too fantastic to be real. For example, he **made predictions** of strange and amazing things that would happen in the future, and many stories claim that he could change himself into different objects and animals. He could change into a boy or a deer, for example, and he could change the appearance of others and even make them invisible. However, there are other parts of the stories we accept more easily, such as the magnificent castle of Camelot with its many towers.

6 There have been various **theories** about where Camelot was located and whether it even existed. In the late 1960s, historians dug at a **site** in southeastern England (Cadbury Castle) where Camelot could have been located, but they found nothing. Some historians say that big stone castles didn't exist in the time of Arthur. Castles during his time were made of dirt and stone, and they were nothing like the castle described in the stories.

7 Still, the idea of Camelot as a wonderful, perfect place continues. In the 1960s, there was a popular musical show called *Camelot* that said that life was perfect in Arthur's castle. Today in the English language, the word *Camelot* has come to mean an ideal place. It is often associated with President John F. Kennedy's White House years, because his presidency started a new "golden age" of **prosperity** in the United States.

8 Most of the stories about King Arthur were written in the ninth century and later. The stories tell us about the people and values of these times. Most of them talk about a code of honor, or chivalry. King Arthur and his knights were all chivalrous. They respected others. A chivalrous person did not kill his enemy after the enemy surrendered. Arthur and his knights were expected to show respect for the church and pity for the poor, as well as bravery and courtesy.

9 The most famous version of King Arthur's legend, a book called *Morte d'Arthur (Death of Arthur),* was written by Sir Thomas Malory in the fifteenth century. In his work, Malory creates a story of extraordinary bravery and emphasizes the triumph of good over evil. This work inspired kings all over Europe. King Henry VIII of England saw himself as the new Arthur reuniting the country after civil war, and even naming his eldest son Arthur.

10 King Arthur's popularity is ongoing. In 1986, it was estimated that 13,500 books, articles, and reviews had been written about him. The success of recent movies and books shows that the popularity of the legend of King Arthur is still strong today. Why is this? The story of Arthur is an adventure story. There are sword fights and wars that make the story exciting. There is also romance, and the setting is far away and **exotic**. The themes in the stories are **universal**: the fight between good and evil, the **conflict** between love and duty. Another theme in the stories shows that although Arthur is a king, he makes mistakes and, like all people, he is not perfect. He is, in fact, like us in many ways. Maybe it is this **combination of** greatness and humanness that has made King Arthur a popular figure around the world and **throughout history**.

VOCABULARY

MEANING

Circle the letter of the answer that is closest in meaning to the underlined word.

1. Arthur returns to the lake and disappears into the <u>mist</u>.
   a. rain
   b. fog
   c. water
   d. storm

2. In the late 1960s, historians dug at a <u>site</u> in southeastern England.
   a. country
   b. place
   c. cave
   d. city

3. The setting is far away and <u>exotic</u>.
   a. familiar and like home
   b. similar to the way things always are
   c. hard to understand
   d. different from the usual

4. There have been various <u>theories</u> about where Camelot was located.
   a. facts
   b. questions
   c. stories
   d. ideas

5. We even <u>encounter</u> them today in books, on television, and in the movies.
   a. discuss
   b. see
   c. carry
   d. like

6. He was the character who <u>inspired</u> hundreds of stories.
   a. was the force behind
   b. caused not to happen
   c. took away from
   d. helped to write

7. They saved young women in trouble and searched for a <u>precious</u> cup.
   a. having great value
   b. being very beautiful
   c. containing lots of decorations
   d. lacking importance

8. One of the themes in the stories is the <u>conflict</u> between love and duty.
   a. agreement
   b. understanding
   c. struggle
   d. change

9. His presidency started a new "golden age" of <u>prosperity</u>.
   a. peace
   b. happiness
   c. pleasure
   d. wealth

10. The themes in the stories are <u>universal</u>.
    a. different in every country
    b. common to a few areas
    c. the same everywhere
    d. unlike anything else

 WORDS THAT GO TOGETHER

A. Find words in the reading that go together with the words below to make phrases.

1. _____ predictions
2. combination _____
3. known _____
4. _____ history
5. _____ deeds
6. passed _____ from
7. _____ trouble

B. Complete the sentences with the phrases from Part A.

1. If you knew someone who _____, she could tell you what is going to happen in the future.
2. Important items and stories that are given by elders to the children in a family are _____ one generation to another.
3. If you take two or more things and put them together, you have a _____ those things.
4. If something is _____ having a certain quality or being a certain way, it means that many people are aware of that fact or characteristic.
5. When something is a certain way over many, many years, it is that way _____.
6. If you are having a serious problem or difficulty, you are _____.
7. To do _____ means to do things that help others.

C. Now use the phrases in your own sentences.

Example: *She was* known as *a very good doctor.*

USE

Work with a partner to answer the questions. Use complete sentences.

1. What are two things that are *precious* to you?
2. What are some common *good deeds* that people can do for others?
3. When was the last time you were *in trouble*? Describe what happened.
4. What is a famous historical *site* in your country?
5. What is something that has been *passed down from* one generation to another in your family?
6. What are some signs of *prosperity*?
7. Where is it common to see *mist*?
8. What *exotic* place would you like to visit?

COMPREHENSION

UNDERSTANDING MAIN IDEAS

Some of the following statements are main ideas, and some are supporting statements. Some of them are stated directly in the reading. Find the statements. Write *M* for each main idea. Write *S* for each supporting statement.

_____ 1. The knights saved people in trouble and searched for the Holy Grail.

_____ 2. The stories about King Arthur contain both truth and fiction.

_____ 3. People have different opinions about whether Camelot existed and where it might have been located.

_____ 4. Many historians believe that Arthur led an army against the Saxons who invaded Britain.

_____ 5. In the English language, the word *Camelot* has come to mean an ideal place.

_____ 6. People from many different times and places have been fascinated by the legends of King Arthur.

REMEMBERING DETAILS

Reread the passage and answer the questions. Write complete sentences.

1. What is the most famous version of King Arthur's legend?

     _____

2. What are three things that were expected of a chivalrous knight?

     _____

3. What did many legends claim about Merlin?

     _____

4. Why did the knights sit at a round table?

     _____

5. What do historians believe that castles were made from during the time of King Arthur?

     _____

6. What is probably one of the reasons why King Arthur has always been such a popular figure?

     _____

7. Where did Arthur get his second magic sword?

     _____

8. During what time do most historians believe that Arthur lived?

     _____

 MAKING INFERENCES

The answers to these questions can be inferred, or guessed, from the reading. Circle the letter of the best answer.

1. The reading implies that _____.
    a. Merlin most likely did exist
    b. Merlin's actions are based in fact
    c. Merlin is not a believable character
    d. Merlin did not live in Camelot

2. It can be inferred from the reading that people many centuries ago _____.

    a. liked stories about love and adventure

    b. didn't believe their heroes should have any faults

    c. were tired of stories about knights and kings

    d. didn't have much imagination

3. From the reading, it can be concluded that Arthur was probably _____.

    a. a person who never really existed in history

    b. a military leader whose real life became exaggerated

    c. several different people who became one character

    d. one of the most famous knights in all of British history

4. The reading implies that the legends of King Arthur _____.

    a. could only be understood by the royalty of their day

    b. caused a civil war during the time of King Henry VIII

    c. showed only the good side of the king and his knights

    d. touched everyone, from kings to ordinary people

DISCUSSION

Discuss the answers to these questions with your classmates.

1. What legends are associated with certain countries?
2. Why do you think people like stories about great heroes? Why are the most popular heroes those who have human faults?
3. Many people say that "chivalry is dead" today. Do you agree? Why or why not?
4. What is your idea of a perfect place like *Camelot*?

WRITING

On separate paper, write a paragraph or an essay about one of the following topics:

1. Write the story of a legend you know.
2. Describe a perfect place to live.
3. Tell about a romantic or adventure movie you have seen.

GRAMMAR AND PUNCTUATION

 SUBJECT-VERB AGREEMENT

1. **A singular subject takes a singular verb, and a plural subject takes a plural verb.**

    Arthur has two magic swords.

    Of course, they always win.

    Two subjects joined by *and* take a plural verb.

    King Arthur and his knights fight for justice and truth.

2. **Words between the subject and the verb do not change subject-verb agreement.**

    The story of King Arthur and the Knights of the Round Table makes us think of an age of romance. (The subject is *the story*, not *King Arthur and the Knights of the Round Table*.)

    Phrases like *together with, as well as,* and *accompanied by* do not change the subject-verb agreement.

    King Arthur, together with his knights, sits at the Round Table.

3. **When a sentence starts with *there*, the verb must agree with the subject that follows.**

    There is also romance.

    There are sword fights.

Underline the correct form of the verb in parentheses.

1. There (is / are) parts of the stories that (is / are) easier to accept.
2. The magnificent castle of Camelot with its many towers (is / are) believable.
3. King Arthur, with his beautiful wife, Guinevere, (live / lives) in Camelot.
4. Sir Lancelot and Sir Gawain (is / are) the most famous knights.
5. King Arthur, together with his knights, always (win / wins) the battle.
6. The stories about Arthur (has / have) some truths.
7. There (has / have) been many theories about where Camelot was located.
8. The most famous version of the stories about King Arthur (was / were) written by Sir Thomas Malory.
9. King Arthur, like all people, (is / are) not perfect.
10. The combination of greatness and humanness (make / makes) King Arthur popular.

UNIT 2

Why Did the Inca Empire Disappear?

BEFORE YOU READ

Answer these questions.

1. Who were the earliest people to settle in your country? What do you know about them?
2. How long ago do you think the Incas lived?
3. In what part of the world do you think the Incas lived?

Why Did the Inca Empire Disappear?

1 The land of the Incas included what is now Bolivia, Peru, Ecuador, and part of Argentina and Chile. In the center of the Inca Empire was its capital, Cuzco, the "Sacred City of the Sun." From every part of the empire, grain, gold and silver, cloth, and food poured into the capital.

2 The Incas began as a small tribe living in the Peruvian Andes in the 1100s. In the 1300s, their strong leader, Mayta Qapaq, began to conquer neighboring lands. By the 1400s, the Incas' huge empire became the largest empire known in the Americas. Although there were only 40,000 Incas, they ruled a population of about 12 million, which included 100 different peoples. The Incas were clever governors and did not always force their own ideas on other groups. The people they conquered had to accept the Inca gods, but they were **allowed** to worship in their own way and keep their own customs.

3 Each new ruler of the empire was called the Sapa Inca, and each Sapa Inca **claimed** to be the child of the sun and was treated as a god. When a Sapa Inca died, his body was kept and taken care of by the people, and he continued to "live" in his palace. The dead Inca sat on a golden stool, and a woman watched him day and night, whisking the flies away from his face. The dead rulers were served food each day, and **on special occasions** they were carried out of their palaces to feast together. Each new ruler had to build a new palace. By 1500, Cuzco was full of palaces of dead Incas.

4 Each Sapa Inca had a queen, or Coya. She was almost always the ruler's own sister. Like him, she was thought to be a child of the sun. The Sapa Inca married his sister to make sure their children only had the pure blood of the sun. One of their sons would be the next Sapa Inca. However, each Sapa Inca had many unofficial wives and dozens of children who would become the Inca nobility.

5 The Incas ruled over one of the best organized empires in history. They controlled the lives of everyone through a system of officials. This system was like a triangle or pyramid. At the bottom were millions of ordinary farmers. Above the farmers were officials and higher officials, and above these officials were the four governors of the quarters of the empire. At the very top of the pyramid was the Sapa Inca.

6 Ordinary people had to spend part of each year working for the state—mining, buildings roads, or **serving in the army**. They could not leave their villages without official permission. They had no choice but to work on the land and send one-third of their produce to the government stores. The empire had huge storehouses where food was kept. The Incas made sure no one **starved**. In return, everyone was expected to work.

7 Even marriage of the ordinary people was controlled. Although nobles often had several wives, an ordinary man could only have one. The state controlled whom and when each ordinary person could marry. Each year the local chiefs assembled all the **eligible** young men over twenty-four and women over eighteen. They were grouped into two lines and then paired together. For the first year of marriage, the couple did not have to pay taxes on either goods or labor. However, they would have to work hard for the rest of their lives. When they were elderly and became too **frail** or sick to take care of themselves, they received free food and clothes from the state storehouse, and their family group would care for them.

8 The Incas had no horses or wheels to help them with transportation, but they had a **sophisticated** road system. Their network of roads ran the length of the empire, from today's Peru to Chile. One road, called the Royal Road, was 3,250 miles (5,200 km) long. It was built through the Andes Mountains. Even today, with modern tools, it would be difficult to build that road. The Incas also made extraordinary suspension bridges of ropes; these hung 300 feet (91 meters) above deep rivers. Since most people were not allowed to travel, the roads were used by soldiers and *chasquis*, who were government messengers. They were highly trained runners who were stationed **at intervals** of about two miles (3.2 km) along the roads and carried messages to and from Cuzco, the capital. Relay teams could run up to 200 miles (322 km) a day and bring fish from the sea to the capital in two days. But the main reason for the roads was for the soldiers who kept the empire **under control**.

9 Although they had no system of writing, the Incas sent messages in *quipus*, which were colored strings with **knots** in them. The color of the string represented what was being counted. For example, a yellow string **stood for** gold and a red string for soldiers. The knots stood for numbers.

10 The Incas were expert builders, although they only had basic tools. Instead of building walls with cement, they used stones that fit together perfectly. Many of the Inca walls remain in place to this day. In 1950,

two-thirds of Cuzco was destroyed in an earthquake, but none of the old walls **collapsed.** Today the well-preserved town of Machu Picchu shows the remarkable skills of the Inca builders. This town, which was **abandoned** by the Incas for unknown reasons, was only discovered in 1911.

11 The Inca Empire fell very quickly after the death of their great ruler Huayna Capac in 1525. Two of his sons, Atahualpa and Huascar, quarreled over who should be the next Sapa Inca. They fought against each other in a war and finally, in 1532, Atahualpa won. During the war, news came that strange people had arrived on the coast. These visitors, the Spaniards, were dressed in metal suits, rode unknown animals (horses), and had hair growing down their chins. After his victory, Atahualpa wanted to see these strange people and invited them to visit him. There were only 180 Spaniards, so Atahualpa was not afraid. However, the Spaniards attacked the Inca army with guns and fired their cannons. They took Atahualpa prisoner and promised to give him his freedom **in exchange for** a room full of gold and two rooms full of silver. The Incas gave the Spaniards the gold and silver. However, the Spaniards didn't free Atahualpa; they killed him instead. With no leader, the Inca soldiers were weak, and the Spaniards soon defeated them. The Spaniards gave the Incas orders, and the Incas obeyed them because they were used to obeying all their lives. The Spaniards were only interested in the Inca gold and silver, so they made the people work in the mines and **neglect** the farming. Many Incas died from overwork and hunger. The great Inca Empire was soon destroyed.

12 Though the Inca civilization disappeared, traces of its culture and people survive. As a matter of fact, today the Incas' descendants form the **majority of** the population in the Andes of Ecuador, Peru, and Bolivia.

VOCABULARY

 MEANING

Circle the letter of the answer that is closest in meaning to the underlined word.

1. The Incas had a <u>sophisticated</u> road system.
    a. not well developed
    b. plain and simple
    c. advanced and complicated
    d. roughly put together

2. Each Sapa Inca <u>claimed</u> to be the child of the sun.
    a. stated as a fact
    b. showed to be untrue
    c. questioned the truth of
    d. demanded to know

3. They were <u>allowed</u> to worship in their own way.
    a. forced
    b. forbidden
    c. told how
    d. given permission

4. They made the people work in the mines and <u>neglect</u> the farming.
    a. not care for
    b. take care of
    c. do more of
    d. watch over

5. Machu Picchu was <u>abandoned</u> by the Incas.
    a. torn down
    b. left empty or alone
    c. made more beautiful
    d. built up

6. The Incas made sure that no one <u>starved</u>.
    a. had food
    b. went without food
    c. was forced to buy food
    d. stored food

7. When they became too <u>frail</u> or sick to take care of themselves, they received free food and clothes.
    a. completely unhappy
    b. lonely and afraid
    c. poor and hungry
    d. thin and weak

8. None of the old Inca walls <u>collapsed</u>.
   a. had large cracks
   b. fell down
   c. were damaged
   d. showed signs of aging

9. Each year the local chiefs assembled all the <u>eligible</u> young men.
   a. very intelligent
   b. physically strong
   c. suitable to be chosen
   d. belonging to a certain class

10. The Incas sent messages in *quipus,* which were colored strings with <u>knots</u> in them.
    a. pieces tied together
    b. long, separate pieces
    c. tiny, loose pieces
    d. pieces hanging from something

WORDS THAT GO TOGETHER

A. Find words in the reading that go together with the words below to make phrases.

1. _____ intervals
2. majority _____
3. on _____ occasions
4. _____ exchange for
5. stood _____
6. _____ in the army
7. _____ control

B. Complete the sentences with the phrases from Part A.

1. When you give something in order to get something else in return, then you give one _____ the other.

2. _____, such as birthdays and weddings, we celebrate important events in our lives.

3. People who are _____ of someone act according to certain rules and laws.

4. The _____ the people is most of the people.

5. You are _____ when you become a member of and spend time working in that part of a country's military.

6. Things that are _____ are spaced certain distances apart from each other.

7. If certain letters or objects represented something else, then they _____ that thing.

C. Now use the phrases in your own sentences.

Example: *The traffic lights changed* at intervals *of two minutes.*

USE

Work with a partner to answer the questions. Use complete sentences.

1. What place was *abandoned* by early people who once lived there?

2. Where have you seen an object, group of letters, or a sign that *stood for* something else? What did it represent?

3. What are some of the characteristics of a *sophisticated* person?

4. In your country, what are the requirements to be *eligible* for marriage?

5. What do you wear *on special occasions* in your country? Talk about two different occasions.

6. What are two things that you are *allowed* to do when you reach a certain age in your family or in your country?

7. What are some things that occur *at intervals* of either time or space?

8. Why shouldn't you *neglect* your work or obligations?

COMPREHENSION

UNDERSTANDING MAIN IDEAS

Circle the letter of the best answer.

1. The main idea of paragraph 2 is that _____.
   a. the Incas allowed conquered people to keep their customs
   b. the first Incas lived in the Peruvian Andes in the 1100s
   c. Mayta Qapaq was a strong Inca leader
   d. a small tribe of Incas grew to a huge empire

2. The main idea of paragraph 5 is that _____.
   a. the Inca government had many officials
   b. the Sapa Inca was at the top of the pyramid
   c. Inca rule was very organized and controlled
   d. the farmers had many people telling them what to do

3. The main idea of paragraph 8 is that _____.
   a. the Inca roads would be hard to build today, even with modern tools
   b. the Inca road system was used mainly by soldiers
   c. most people were not allowed to travel in Inca society
   d. the Incas built a very advanced and complex system of roads

4. Paragraph 11 is mainly about how _____.
   a. the death of Huayna Capac led to war between his two sons
   b. the great Inca Empire was destroyed by the Spaniards
   c. the Spaniards were only interested in Inca gold and silver
   d. Atahualpa was not afraid of the Spaniards

REMEMBERING DETAILS

Reread the passage and fill in the blanks.

1. One Inca road, called the _____, was 3,250 miles (5,200 km) long.

2. For their first year of marriage, a couple did not have to pay _____.

3. In *quipus,* a yellow string stood for _____, a red string stood for _____, and the knots stood for _____.

4. Farmers had to send _____ to government stores.

5. The Spaniards promised Atahualpa his freedom in exchange for _____.

6. The Sapa Inca claimed to be _____.

7. The job of the *chasquis* was to _____ to and from Cuzco.

8. The Incas had amazing suspension bridges made from _____.

MAKING INFERENCES

The answers to these questions are not directly stated in the article. Write complete sentences.

1. What can you conclude about the Inca rulers from the statement that grain, gold, silver, cloth, and food poured into the capital from every part of the empire?

   _____

2. What did the Incas probably believe about their dead rulers?

   _____

3. What can be inferred about the Incas' attitude toward the elderly?

   _____

4. What can you conclude about the lives of the ordinary people in the Inca Empire?

   _____

5. Why do you suppose the Inca governors did not force their ideas on other groups?

   _____

6. What can you infer from the fact that nobles could have several wives but an ordinary man could only have one?

   _____

7. What do the Inca roads, buildings, and walls tell us about the Inca people?

   _____

8. What terrible mistake did Atahualpa make?

   _____

DISCUSSION

Discuss the answers to these questions with your classmates.

1. Why did the Spaniards so easily defeat the Incas? Do you think there was any possibility that the Incas could have won?

2. Why do you think the Incas abandoned Machu Picchu?

3. What are some of the good points about the Inca system of government? What are some of the bad points?

4. Were the Spaniards wise leaders like the Incas were when they conquered people? Explain your answer.

WRITING

On separate paper, write a paragraph or an essay about one of the following topics:

1. What are two advantages and two disadvantages of living in an organized and controlled society such as the society of the Incas?

2. Each country is different and has its own way of doing things. Write about two or three things that are done differently in another country.

3. Who should take care of the elderly? Write the advantages and / or disadvantages of the government's taking care of the elderly.

GRAMMAR AND PUNCTUATION

COMMAS: WITH TRANSITIONAL EXPRESSIONS—*HOWEVER, FOR EXAMPLE, THEREFORE, AS A MATTER OF FACT*

> We use transitional expressions to act as a bridge between one sentence and another, and between parts of a sentence. Transitional expressions can be used at the beginning, in the middle, or at the end of a sentence. We set them off with commas.
>
> *For the first year, the couple did not pay taxes.* **However,** *they would have to work hard for the rest of their lives.*
>
> *For the first year, the couple did not pay taxes. They would have to work hard,* **however,** *for the rest of their lives.*

A. Add commas to the following sentences where necessary.

1. The Incas conquered many different peoples in South America. However they allowed them to keep their own customs.

2. There were huge storehouses all over the country. Therefore no one starved.

3. The roads were used by government messengers. The main reason for the roads however was for the soldiers to keep the empire under control.

4. The Royal Road is a great achievement. As a matter of fact it would be difficult to build even today.

5. The colors on the *quipus* represented what was being counted. Yellow for example stood for gold.

B. Connect the two sentences with a transitional expression.

1. The Spaniards were only interested in the gold and silver of the Incas. They made the people work in mines and neglected the farming.

    _____

    _____

2. Ordinary people had no freedom to go where they liked. They could not leave their village without permission.

    _____

    _____

UNIT 3

How Do Hindus Celebrate the Diwali Festival?

BEFORE YOU READ

Answer these questions.

1. What is your favorite holiday? Why?
2. What special things do you do to celebrate the holiday?
3. How long do the celebrations last?

How Do Hindus Celebrate the Diwali Festival?

1 Diwali is the Hindu festival of light. The Hindus in India celebrate their favorite festival on the dark and cold nights of late October or early November. *Diwali*, which is **short for** *dipawali*, means "row of lights." There are lights everywhere during this festival, which is as important to Hindus as Christmas is to Christians. Houses have lights in front of their doors and windows, the streets are decorated with lights, and the temples have tiny **rows of** lights all over. Diwali, which lasts for five days, is one of the longest festivals for Hindus. In India, it's a time when everything stops. Families get together, eat together, and exchange gifts, usually of candies. They go shopping and buy things, from new clothes to new homes.

2 As with other Indian festivals, Diwali has different **significance** for people in various parts of India, **depending upon** which gods the people worship at this time. However, the basic reason for this festival is the same all over India: Diwali is a time for new beginnings. It is a time when light **triumphs** over darkness and good triumphs over evil.

3 Before celebrating Diwali, Hindus prepare and decorate their homes. People **make sure that** their houses are **spotless**. Every house is repainted and **thoroughly** cleaned. They decorate the floors and sidewalks outside their homes with special *rangoli* patterns to welcome guests. *Rangoli* means "a mixture of colors." The patterns are created from a paste made from rice flour. The paste is usually colored red or yellow. The Hindus believe red and yellow make the evil spirits go away. One traditional Hindu pattern is the lotus flower, which is the symbol of one of their gods, *Lakshmi*.

4 Lights play an important part in the Diwali festival. Weeks before the festival, potters make clay lamps called *diwas*. On the first day of Diwali, every family buys a new lamp, which symbolizes new beginnings. There are lights everywhere in the streets. Even in parts of India where there is no electricity, thousands of these clay lamps can be seen. The lamps welcome travelers and help visitors find the houses they are going to visit. They are also there so the gods that people are remembering will see the lights and **pay** them **a visit**. In addition to light, there is noise—the noise of firecrackers. Families spend a lot of money on firecrackers and light them for four or five hours at night in their backyards and gardens. At the end of Diwali, there are also big fireworks **displays** that light up the sky.

5 Hindus start every day of Diwali by taking a bath. After their baths, family members will rub scented oils into each other's hair. Then they get dressed in new clothes for the festival. Women will wear lots of jewelry and may draw special patterns on their hands and feet with henna. Then they pray at the family **shrine**. Every Hindu home has a shrine with pictures and statues of different gods. The shrine is usually in the living room of the house, where it is easy to get together every day and pray. After they pray at the shrine, they go out and visit family, friends, and business **colleagues**. They take gifts with them of candies and dry fruits. They believe if you give sweet things, people will think sweet things about you. Some people may go to the market where there are stalls selling sweets, flowers, and jewelry. There's also village dancing, and everyone can join in. At the end of the day, they all go home to eat and light fireworks.

6 Diwali is a time when people look forward to good luck and wealth in the year to come. The Hindu goddess of wealth, *Lakshmi*, is **honored** during the festival. People hope that a visit from this goddess will bring them good luck. To help Lakshmi enter their homes, they leave all the windows and doors open and make sure there are lights shining at every door and window so that she can find her way in easily. Businesspeople put out all their account books for Lakshmi to inspect. Hindus pay their bills and leave money and jewelry on the shrine to her in their house.

7 In western India, Diwali starts the new business year. There is a ceremony of closing the account books and showing them to Lakshmi. Businesspeople who **take part in** the ceremony have red marks on their foreheads. During Diwali, people always visit their coworkers and send "Happy Diwali" cards and exchange gifts.

8 Hindus in other parts of the world also celebrate Diwali. Outside India, the temple is more important in the festivities than the home is. This is because Diwali is not a long public holiday in other countries, and Hindus have to go to work as usual. The temple is a good place for them to meet for the festivities. Outside India, Hindus usually spend their whole day in the temple, whereas in India they would go there to pray to the gods and then go home. In the temple during Diwali, the priests dress the figures of the gods in brightly colored silk clothes to receive their visitors. When visitors come, they ring the temple bell to **let** the gods **know** that they have arrived, and they bring gifts of sweets and flowers. The temple is usually covered with offerings of sweets, flowers, fruit, and cakes. People bring food not only for the gods but also for themselves.

Everybody eats and listens to traditional music. There are no **formal** religious services, but every visitor says a private prayer to the gods and asks for good fortune.

9 Diwali is a time to be happy and enjoy family and friends. It's a time when people exchange sweets, wear their new clothes, buy jewelry, and have a festive time. However, for the Hindus, Diwali is more than eating and shopping. Its burning lamp is a message of peace and **harmony** to the world.

VOCABULARY

 MEANING

Circle the letter of the answer that is closest in meaning to the underlined word.

1. They <u>thoroughly</u> clean their houses.
   a. partly
   b. mostly
   c. completely
   d. generally

2. There are no <u>formal</u> religious services.
   a. not like any other
   b. official
   c. taking a long time
   d. taking place every day

3. In various parts of India, different gods are <u>honored</u>.
   a. showed praise and respect
   b. asked a favor of
   c. given special names
   d. talked about by everyone

4. The burning lamp is a message of peace and <u>harmony</u>.
   a. acting according to reason
   b. having a great love for other people
   c. being quiet and restful
   d. being in agreement with others

5. They pray at the family <u>shrine</u>.

    a. a kind of ceremony

    b. a place for worship

    c. an area for entertainment

    d. an important meal

6. They make sure their houses are <u>spotless</u>.

    a. almost empty

    b. very bright

    c. like new

    d. completely clean

7. It is a time when light <u>triumphs</u> over darkness.

    a. tries to control

    b. wins a victory

    c. has a strong feeling against

    d. makes better

8. They visit business <u>colleagues</u>.

    a. people who work together

    b. people who play on the same sports team

    c. people who are wealthy

    d. family members

9. Diwali has different <u>significance</u> for people in various parts of India.

    a. history and customs

    b. type of ceremony

    c. importance and meaning

    d. time and place

10. There are fireworks <u>displays</u> that light up the sky.

    a. shows that people see

    b. songs that people sing

    c. noises that people hear

    d. ceremonies that people take part in

WORDS THAT GO TOGETHER

A. Find words in the reading that go together with the words below to make phrases.

1. _____ . . . know
2. _____ . . . a visit
3. take part _____
4. rows _____
5. _____ sure that
6. depending _____
7. short _____

B. Complete the sentences with the phrases from Part A.

1. When you have _____ things, they are arranged side by side in a line.

2. When you _____ people _____, you go to see them and spend time with them.

3. If one thing may change because of something else, it is _____ something else.

4. If you _____ a person _____ about something, you tell them about it.

5. When you use part of a word instead of the whole word, then the smaller word is _____ the larger one.

6. When you _____ something happens, you do everything you can to be certain that it does happen.

7. When you do something with other people, you _____ that activity.

C. Now use the phrases in your own sentences.

Example: *I let* my friend *know* about the free concert tickets.

USE

Work with a partner to answer the questions. Use complete sentences.

1. What is the name of a famous *shrine*? Where is it? Why is it famous?
2. What is the *significance* of a white dress in your culture?
3. Where can you find *rows of* chairs?
4. Which people are *honored* in your country? Why are they honored?

5. If you could *pay* someone famous *a visit*, who would you choose to see?

6. In your culture, what type of clothing is *formal*?

7. What happens when people don't live in *harmony*?

8. What are some words that you use every day that are *short for* other words?

COMPREHENSION

UNDERSTANDING MAIN IDEAS

Some of the following statements are main ideas, and some are supporting statements. Some of them are stated directly in the reading. Find the statements. Write *M* for each main idea. Write *S* for each supporting statement.

_____ 1. Diwali, which lasts for five days, is one of the longest festivals for Hindus.

_____ 2. Lights play an important part in the Diwali festival.

_____ 3. Diwali is a time when people look forward to good luck and wealth in the year to come.

_____ 4. Businesspeople who take part in the ceremony have red marks on their foreheads.

_____ 5. Hindus in other parts of the world also celebrate Diwali.

REMEMBERING DETAILS

Reread the passage and answer the questions. Write complete sentences.

1. How do Hindus start every day of Diwali?

_____

2. What does *rangoli* mean?

_____

3. During Diwali, what decorates the windows and doors of houses?

_____

4. What do family members do after they pray at the shrine?

_____

5. In the temple, how do the priests dress the figures of the gods?

_____

6. What colors do the Hindus believe make the evil spirits go away?

_____

7. During Diwali, what does a new lamp symbolize?

_____

8. *Lakshmi* is the goddess of what?

_____

MAKING INFERENCES

The answers to these questions can be inferred, or guessed, from the reading. Circle the letter of the best answer.

1. The reading implies that the Diwali festival _____.
   a. is celebrated in the same way by all Hindus
   b. is a time for family and friends to get together
   c. makes many people wealthy
   d. is a good time for praying alone and having quiet thoughts

2. It can be inferred from the reading that the festival is celebrated with _____.
   a. a belief in the importance of the past
   b. a sense of sorrow for one's mistakes
   c. a spirit of hope for the future
   d. a joy in showing off one's wealth

3. From the reading, it can be concluded that Hindus _____.
   a. work hard to prepare for the festival
   b. don't believe in praying for good luck
   c. celebrate Diwali mostly in their homes
   d. dress very plainly during the festival

4. The reading implies that Diwali is a time for _____.
   a. working hard at your job
   b. going to bed early and getting lots of rest
   c. staying home and praying
   d. doing good things for others

DISCUSSION

Discuss the answers to these questions with your classmates.

1. Why are holidays and festivals important to societies?
2. Many colors have special meanings or create certain feelings when we look at them. Name three colors and what they symbolize. What is your favorite color? Why?
3. All countries have their own customs. What is one custom that you like? What is one that you don't like? Explain your reasons.
4. Food is an important part of many festivals. Why do you think it is?

WRITING

On separate paper, write a paragraph or an essay about one of the following topics:

1. Write about your favorite holiday and how it is celebrated in your country.
2. Write about two or three customs that you like. Give reasons why you like them.
3. Sometimes a festival you know is celebrated differently in another country. Compare and/or contrast the similarities and differences of a festival celebrated in another country.

GRAMMAR AND PUNCTUATION

DIRECT AND INDIRECT SPEECH

We use quotation marks for direct speech (a person's exact words). We use quotation marks at the beginning and at the end of each part of a direct quotation. We put punctuation inside the second pair of quotation marks. We do not use quotation marks for reported, or indirect, speech.

The woman said, "We must keep the tradition alive outside India."
(direct speech)

"We must," the woman said, "keep the tradition alive outside India."
(direct speech)

The woman said that they had to keep the tradition alive outside India.
(indirect speech)

Write *C* for correct sentences. Rewrite the incorrect sentences with correct punctuation.

_____ 1. The woman said that "there were statues of different gods in the shrine."

_____

_____ 2. He told us that Hindus usually end their meal with *lassi*.

_____

_____ 3. The woman said, "Guests who visit between mealtimes receive special snacks."

_____

_____ 4. "The symbol of Lakshmi, she said, is a lotus flower."

_____

_____ 5. He said that today they are putting metal lamps on their shrines.

_____

_____ 6. Spices she said are the essence of Indian cuisine.

_____

_____ 7. "Lots of foods, including special sweets, are eaten together on a special plate called a *thali*, she said.

_____

UNIT 4

What Is the Story Behind *The 1,001 Arabian Nights?*

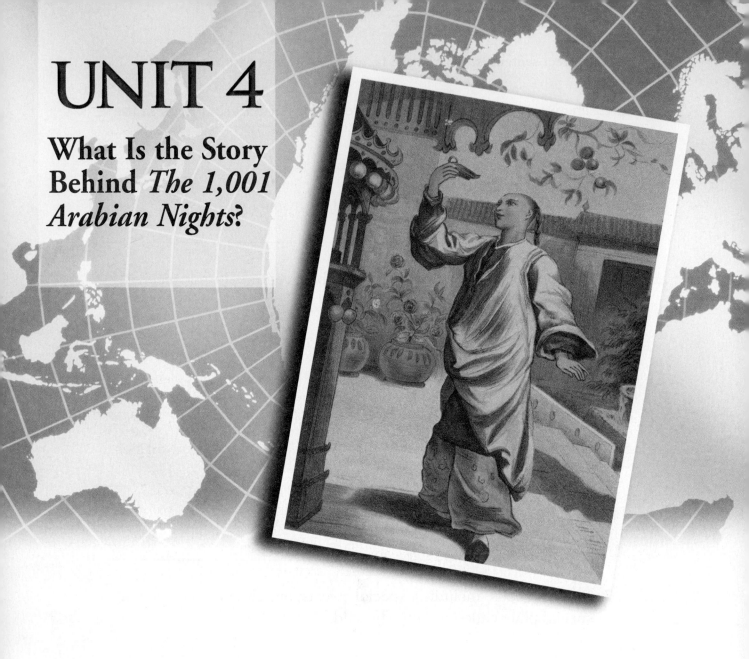

BEFORE YOU READ

Answer these questions.

1. What kinds of stories do you like? Adventure? Mystery? Romance?
2. What are some famous stories or folktales?
3. Which stories are popular in your country?

What Is the Story Behind
The 1,001 Arabian Nights?

1 *The 1,001 Arabian Nights,* also known as *The Book of One Thousand and One Nights,* is one of the most famous pieces of Arabic literature. It includes many well-known stories, such as "Ali Baba and the Forty Thieves," "Sinbad the Sailor," and "Aladdin's Lamp." In all, the collection of stories contains about 200 folk tales from Arabia, India, Persia (modern day Iran), and even China. Many people in these countries shared a religion, Islam, and the Arabic language of the Koran.

2 These stories are very ancient and are believed to first have been told by an Arab storyteller in the ninth century. There are various types of stories: love stories, historical tales, comedies, tragedies, poems, and religious legends. The stories **depict** what life was like at the time and include good and bad rulers, magicians, and lots of adventure. The stories have been told and retold for generations. Later on, in the Middle Ages, a "frame" to all these stories was added. The frame for the large group of stories is the story of Sherezade. In her tale, she tells many of *The 1,001 Arabian Nights* stories.

3 The story of Sherezade begins with the tale of a king named Shahryar who rules an unnamed island "between India and China." Shahryar had a wife whom he loved more than anything in the world. He was **devoted to** her and would do anything for her. However, after several years, he discovered completely by accident that she had been **unfaithful** to him. **Betrayed**, the King **carried out** the law of the land and ordered his chief minister to put her to death. Then the heartbroken king **went out of his mind** and declared that all women were unfaithful like his wife. The fewer there were of them, he thought, the better the world would be. So every evening he married a new wife and commanded that she be **executed** the following morning.

4 It was job of the chief minister to provide the king with these unfortunate brides. The chief minister did his duty with great **reluctance**, for it was hard for him to see a woman married one day and then killed the next. The people of the town lived in sadness and fear. Fathers and mothers cried about the fate of their daughters. The chief minister himself had two daughters: Sherezade and Dinarzade. Sherezade was older; she was a clever and brave girl. Her father had given her the best education, and she was one of the most beautiful girls in the kingdom.

5 One day, Sherezade asked her father a favor. Her father loved her very much, and he would not refuse her anything that was reasonable. Sherezade then told him that she was determined to end the cruel practice of the king. She had a plan to save the women of the kingdom from their terrible fate. Since her father had to provide the king with a new wife every day, she **implored** him to choose her. Her father was shocked by her request and thought she had **lost her senses**. But Sherezade explained that if her plan succeeded, she would **do a** great **service for** her country. After she begged and begged him, her father finally agreed to Sherezade's wish. He went to the palace to tell the king that the following evening he would bring him Sherezade to be the new queen. The **astonished** king asked him why he would sacrifice his own daughter. The chief minister replied that it was her wish. The king then told the minister to bring his daughter to the palace.

6 When her father returned to tell her, Sherezade was happy and thanked her father for agreeing to her wish. She then went to prepare herself for the marriage. But, first, she wanted to speak with her sister, Dinarzade. Sherezade told her sister that she had a plan and needed her help. She said her father was going to take her to the palace to celebrate her marriage with the king. As a final wish, she would ask the king to let her sister sleep in their bedroom during the last night that she was alive. If the king **granted** her wish, which she hoped he would, then Dinarzade should wake her up an hour before daybreak and say these words to her, "My sister, if you are not asleep, please tell me one of your charming stories." Then Sherezade would begin to tell a tale, and she hoped by this to save the people from their terrible fate. Dinarzade said she would do what her sister asked of her.

7 When the time for the marriage came, the chief minister took Sherezade to the palace and left her alone with the king. The king told her to raise her veil and was amazed at her beauty. But Sherezade had tears in her eyes. When the king asked what was the matter, Sherezade said that she had a sister whom she loved very much, and she asked the king if he would allow her sister to spend the night in the same room since it would be the last time they would be together. The king agreed to her wish.

8 An hour before daybreak, Dinarzade woke up and asked Sherezade, "My sister, if you are not asleep, please tell me one of your charming stories before the sun rises. It is the last time I'll have the pleasure of

hearing you." Sherezade asked the king if he would let her do as her sister requested. "Of course," answered the king. So Sherezade began to tell the king a story. But when she reached the most exciting part of it, she stopped. She said that if he wanted to hear the end he would have to let her live another day. Each night she would tell him a story, ending at daybreak with a "cliff hanger"—leaving off at an exciting part.

9 The enchanted king always wanted to hear the rest of the story, and so he **put off** her death night after night. He was **dazzled** by her thrilling stories, and soon he fell in love with her. Sherezade was able to **spin a** new **tale** for 1,001 nights. By this time, she had given birth to three sons, and the king became convinced of her faithfulness. Sherezade's plan was successful, and all the people **rejoiced** because the women in the kingdom were saved.

VOCABULARY

MEANING

Circle the letter of the answer that is closest in meaning to the underlined word.

1. The chief minister did his duty with great <u>reluctance</u>.
   a. fear
   b. unwillingness
   c. eagerness
   d. carelessness

2. Sherezade <u>implored</u> her father to choose her.
   a. begged
   b. helped
   c. screamed at
   d. refused

3. The people <u>rejoiced</u> because the women were saved.
   a. celebrated
   b. relaxed
   c. complained
   d. laughed

4. The stories <u>depict</u> what life was like at the time.
   a. create
   b. copy
   c. show
   d. question

5. The king's wife was <u>unfaithful</u>.
   a. jealous of him
   b. untrue to him
   c. confused by him
   d. honest with him

6. The king was <u>dazzled</u> by Sherezade's stories.
   a. tired
   b. angered
   c. confused
   d. amazed

7. The king commanded that every new wife be <u>executed</u> in the morning.
   a. punished
   b. beaten
   c. killed
   d. sent away

8. The <u>astonished</u> king asked Sherezade's father why he would sacrifice his daughter.
   a. angry
   b. worried
   c. surprised
   d. eager

9. The king <u>granted</u> Sherezade's wish.
   a. refused
   b. allowed
   c. understood
   d. returned

10. The king was <u>betrayed</u> by his wife.
   a. warned
   b. controlled
   c. treated dishonestly
   d. not taken care of

 WORDS THAT GO TOGETHER

A. Find words in the reading that go together with the words below to make phrases.

1. went out of his _____

2. _____ a service _____

3. carried _____

4. spin a _____

5. _____ her senses

6. devoted _____

7. _____ off

B. Complete the sentences with the phrases from Part A.

1. A person who makes up stories knows how to _____ _____.

2. When something is accomplished or a rule is followed, it is
    _____.

3. If a man was so upset that he acted unreasonably, you might say that he
    _____.

4. When you _____ something, you delay it or make it
    wait until a later time.

5. If you are _____ someone or something, it means that
    you love and give great importance to that person or thing.

6. When you help people, you _____ them.

7. If a woman did something crazy and unusual, her friends might think
    that she had _____.

C. Now use the phrases in your own sentences.

Example: *The manager watched his workers to make sure they* carried out
        his requests.

USE

Work with a partner to answer the questions. Use complete sentences.

1. Besides folktales, what else might *depict* what life was like in the past?

2. Has anyone ever *granted* a wish for you? What was your wish?

3. What are two historical events that *astonished* you?

4. What career would be good for someone who can *spin a tale*?

5. Have you experienced a situation where people *rejoiced*? What were some of the things they did to celebrate?

6. Who is a famous person in history who was *betrayed*?

7. Where might you be *dazzled* by what you see or hear?

8. Would you like to *do a service for* your country? What type of service?

COMPREHENSION

UNDERSTANDING MAIN IDEAS

Circle the letter of the best answer.

1. The main idea of paragraph 2 is that _____.
   a. the frame for many of the tales is the story of Sherezade
   b. the stories were told in the ninth century
   c. the book is made up of many ancient stories
   d. the tales tell us about the past

2. The main idea of paragraph 5 is that _____.
   a. Sherezade's father loved her very much
   b. Sherezade wanted to marry the king in order to help her country
   c. both the king and Sherezade's father were shocked by her wish to marry
   d. Sherezade had to beg her father to let her marry the king

3. Paragraph 6 is mainly about Sherezade's _____.
   a. happiness over her father's decision
   b. wish to have her sister with her
   c. marriage to the king
   d. plan to save the women

4. The main idea of paragraph 8 is that _____.

    a. Sherezade used stories to keep the king from executing her

    b. Dinarzade helped to save Sherezade's life

    c. Sherezade ended her story every night

    d. the king was kind to Sherezade and her sister, Dinarzade

REMEMBERING DETAILS

Reread the passage and fill in the blanks.

1. The stories in *The 1,001 Arabian Nights* are from many countries, including _____, _____, _____, and _____.

2. The various kinds of stories in the book are _____, _____, _____, _____, _____, and _____.

3. The king believed that all women were _____.

4. It was the job of the chief minister to provide the king with _____.

5. When the king raised Sherezade's veil, he was amazed by _____.

6. As Sherezade's last wish, she asked the king to _____.

7. In the morning, Dinarzade asked Sherezade to _____.

8. The king put off Sherezade's death night after night because _____.

MAKING INFERENCES

Some of the following statements are facts from the reading. Other statements can be inferred, or guessed. Write *F* for each factual statement. Write *I* for each inference.

_____ 1. *The 1,001 Arabian Nights* is one of the most famous books of Arabic literature.

_____ 2. The stories have been passed down through many generations.

_____ 3. The people of early times loved adventure stories just as people do today.

_____ 4. After the king learned of his wife's unfaithfulness, he was afraid to ever love another woman.

_____ 5. The townspeople cried because their daughters were being executed.

_____ 6. It was a great act of courage for Sherezade to marry the king.

_____ 7. Sherezade's father would not refuse any reasonable wish of hers.

_____ 8. Dinarzade was a loving and faithful sister.

_____ 9. Sherezade was intelligent and understood human nature.

_____10. The people were overjoyed when the king fell in love with Sherezade.

DISCUSSION

Discuss the answers to these questions with your classmates.

1. People have been telling stories throughout history. Why has storytelling always been important to people and societies? How were stories passed down in ancient times? How are they told today?

2. What are the qualities of a hero? What qualities did Sherezade possess?

3. The king believed that because his wife was unfaithful, all women were unfaithful. This is called a _generalization_. Give examples of other generalizations that occur in the world today. How can they create problems?

4. Sometimes friends or coworkers can betray each other, too. Describe this type of betrayal. What problems can it cause?

WRITING

On separate paper, write a paragraph or an essay about one of the following topics:

1. Describe a famous folktale or story that you know.

2. Who do you think has the qualities of a hero? The person can be living or dead. Give reasons.

3. Write about three marriage customs in your country. Give details for each.

GRAMMAR AND PUNCTUATION

 PARTICIPIAL ADJECTIVES

Participial adjectives are formed from the present and past participles of verbs. We use participles of verbs as adjectives: *charming / charmed; thrilling / thrilled; astonishing / astonished.*

1. **The present participle acts as an adjective with an active meaning. These adjectives end in *–ing* and describe someone or something that <u>causes</u> a feeling or reaction.**

   *Please tell me one of your **charming** stories before the sun rises.*

2. **The past participle acts as an adjective with a passive meaning. These adjectives end in *–ed* and describe someone or something that <u>experiences</u> a feeling or reaction.**

   *Dinarzade was **charmed** by the stories.*

Complete the sentences. Use participial adjectives formed by adding *–ing* or *–ed* to the verbs in parentheses. Be careful! Sometimes there are spelling changes to the verb when we form participial adjectives.

1. The king looked forward to her _____ stories. (thrill)

2. The _____ king wanted to hear the end of the story. (dazzle)

3. Sherazade stopped at the most _____ part of the story. (excite)

4. The daughters in the town were _____. (frighten)

5. Sherazade's father was _____ to hear the news that his daughter wanted to marry the king. (shock)

6. The king was _____ that his minister would sacrifice his own daughter. (surprise)

7. There are many _____ stories in *The 1,001 Arabian Nights*. (amuse)

8. The story of Sinbad the Sailor is _____. (enchant)

9. King Shahryar was _____ to his wife. (devote)

10. The king thought Sherazade's beauty was _____. (amaze)

UNIT 5

Who Were the Samurai?

BEFORE YOU READ

Answer these questions.

1. What do you know about the samurai?
2. Have you ever seen a movie about the samurai? If so, did you like it? Why or why not?
3. What people, past or present, were famous for their fighting skills in your country? How did they live? What accomplishments made them famous?

42

Who Were the Samurai?

1 The samurai were warriors, or fearless soldiers, who became powerful in Japan around the 1200s. The samurai, which means "those who serve," were hired by lords to fight their wars and protect their land. The samurai were expert fighters; they were skilled with the sword and the bow and arrow, and they were superior horsemen. They were athletic and strong, and they developed their fighting skills into what is the **basis of** modern **martial arts**.

2 The samurai had a **code of ethics** called *Bushido*, which meant "way of the warrior." The samurai had to have unquestionable **loyalty** to the emperor and their lord (the *daimyo*). They were trustworthy, honest, and kind and generous to the poor. They led **frugal** lives and had no interest in wealth or **material things**. They were only interested in honor and pride. Additionally, they had to be men of **noble spirit** who were not afraid to die, because death in battle only meant honor to their lord and family. If samurai lost a battle or a fight, they would have to commit suicide rather than face dishonor.

3 The samurai developed a special way of dressing. They wore their hair tied back in a top-knot, and their **brow** and crown were shaved. Samurai wore simple clothes when they were not fighting. However, when they were fighting they wore a suit of armor that was made from leather or iron strips so it was completely flexible. Their most important weapon and sign of their class was a pair of matching swords. Only samurai had the right to carry swords. They believed that swords had special powers. The people who made swords were master craftsmen, and to this day people can tell who created the sword of a samurai by the way the blade was made.

4 The wives of the samurai followed the same code of ethics as the men did. Since the **privileges** and rights of the samurai were passed down from father to son, it was important for a wife to have a male child. Sometimes a samurai took another wife if the first wife did not give birth to a son. Samurai women were trained fighters like their husbands. They kept a short knife in a piece of silk material they wrapped around their waist. They also were trained to use long, curved swords. In times of war, they fought to defend their homes and sometimes joined the men in battle.

5 In the beginning, samurai women were very independent. However, after the 1600s, they had to follow the religious beliefs of that time. These beliefs included the teachings of the "Three Obediences." This stated that

a woman had no independence through life. When she was young, she obeyed her father; when she married, she obeyed her husband; when she was widowed, she obeyed her son. Samurai women are remembered as being courageous, no matter what they suffered. Today, a play is still performed in Japan about two brave samurai sisters who fought to avenge their father's death.

6 Until the 1600s, the samurai belonged to a special class of people that fought and farmed the land they lived on. However, during the Edo period (1600s–1867), their **status** and way of life changed. Japan had become a peaceful country, and its rulers didn't want the samurai to fight anymore. They made the samurai live permanently in castles, paid them with rice, and gave them many special rights. Though some samurai worked for the government, many others lived the relaxed life of the upper class. During this time, some samurai helped create the forms of art that we consider to be typically Japanese. These include haiku poetry, the *No* style of drama, the tea ceremony, and flower arranging.

7 Around 1867, the leadership and government changed in Japan. The emperor **once again** became the ruler of the country. The lords were ordered to give their land to the emperor, and in return they received money from the state. In 1871, the samurai class was **abolished**. The samurai had lost their land and status; some did not know how to survive.

8 In 1877, some of the unhappy samurai formed a group to fight the emperor. Even though loyalty to the emperor was the highest of samurai values, these warriors felt that they had to fight in order to protect their culture and the future of all samurai people. A samurai called Saigo Takamori led twenty thousand samurai **rebels** against sixty thousand government soldiers. The government had a modern army with modern weapons. The samurai were brave fighters, but their weapons were **inferior**. They lost battle after battle, and finally Saigo and his remaining group went into the hills. They knew they had no chance; nevertheless, they fought to the end. Saigo was wounded and committed suicide in the samurai tradition. Later, Saigo Takamori, now known as "the last samurai," became a hero for the Japanese. Today, the descendants of the samurai have high **esteem** among the Japanese, although they have no official status.

9 Although the Japanese government and society have gone through many changes since the time of the samurai, Bushido values have continued in different forms. After World War II, Japan no longer had an army. It became a modern, **industrialized** country with huge companies.

These companies were like families, and loyalty to one's company and company name was important. Even today, workers for these companies have great respect for their bosses. They do not want to do anything wrong that would bring shame to their company, themselves, or their family. Such loyalty and respect for country, leaders, and family is one example of the continuing **influence of** the great samurai warriors on Japanese society. Though the samurai culture has disappeared, important parts of it live on in this way.

VOCABULARY

 MEANING

Circle the letter of the answer that is closest in meaning to the underlined word.

1. The <u>privileges</u> and rights of the samurai were passed down from father to son.
   - a. important duties
   - b. valuable items
   - c. special favors
   - d. certain abilities

2. The samurai had to have unquestionable <u>loyalty</u> to the emperor.
   - a. faithfulness
   - b. honesty
   - c. admiration
   - d. respect

3. Saigo Takamori led twenty thousand samurai <u>rebels</u>.
   - a. people who oppose authority
   - b. people who are unkind
   - c. people who want to control others
   - d. people who are faithful

4. The samurai led <u>frugal</u> lives.
   - a. comfortable
   - b. requiring little
   - c. expensive
   - d. hidden

5. Today, the descendants of the samurai have high <u>esteem</u> among the Japanese.
   - a. wealth
   - b. titles
   - c. respect
   - d. power

6. Their <u>brow</u> and crown were shaved.
   a. side of the head
   b. front of the head
   c. back of the head
   d. top of the head

7. Their weapons were <u>inferior</u> to those of the government soldiers.
   a. not as many as
   b. not as large as
   c. not as new as
   d. not as good as

8. During the Edo period (1600s–1867), their <u>status</u> and way of life changed.
   a. place to live
   b. responsibilities to others
   c. rights as a citizen
   d. position in society

9. In 1871, the samurai class was <u>abolished</u>.
   a. brought to an end
   b. given high honors
   c. given special advantages
   d. created again

10. Japan became a modern, <u>industrialized</u> country.
    a. having a lot of farms
    b. having many factories and businesses
    c. having many cars and roads
    d. having a large system of government

WORDS THAT GO TOGETHER

A. Find words in the reading that go together with the words below to make phrases.

1. _____ again
2. noble _____
3. _____ things
4. influence _____
5. _____ of ethics
6. martial _____
7. basis _____

B. Complete the sentences with the phrases from Part A.

1. The traditional forms of East Asian self-defense or fighting are known as the _____.
2. If you repeat an action, you do it _____.
3. The _____ something is that from which it is made, started, or built.

4. Possessions and objects are _____; many people believe the mind and spirit are more important.

5. Someone with dignity, bravery, and virtue is thought to have a

_____.

6. The _____ someone or something is its effect on others.

7. A _____ is a system of moral behavior that people live by.

C. Now use the phrases in your own sentences.

Example: *The boy's parents were worried about the* influence of *computer games on his schoolwork.*

USE

Work with a partner to answer the questions. Use complete sentences.

1. Who is a famous person, past or present, who has a *noble spirit*?

2. What *material things* are important to you?

3. Should famous or important people have special *privileges*? Why or why not?

4. Who is or was famous for his or her skill in *martial arts*?

5. If you had the power to change things, what would you like *abolished*?

6. What kind of people are held in high *esteem* in your country or culture?

7. What is something that you would like to do and something that you would not like to do *once again*?

8. What are the names of two groups of people that have a high *status* in your country?

COMPREHENSION

UNDERSTANDING MAIN IDEAS

Some of the following statements are main ideas, and some are supporting statements. Some of them are stated directly in the reading. Find the statements in the reading. Write *M* for each main idea. Write *S* for each supporting statement.

_____ 1. The samurai had a code of ethics called *Bushido,* which meant "way of the warrior."

_____ 2. During the Edo period (1600s–1867), the status and way of life of the samurai changed.

_____ 3. The most important weapon and sign of the samurai class was a pair of matching swords.

_____ 4. Saigo Takamori, now known as "the last samurai," became a hero for the Japanese.

_____ 5. Although the Japanese government and society have gone through many changes since the time of the samurai, Bushido values have continued in different forms.

_____ 6. The Japanese workers do not want to do anything wrong that would bring shame to their company, themselves, or their family.

REMEMBERING DETAILS

Reread the passage and circle the letter of the best answer.

1. In the late 1800s, when the emperor again became the ruler, the samurai class was _____.
   a. abolished
   b. ordered to give land to the emperor
   c. given special rights
   d. moved to castles

2. The code of ethics called *Bushido* meant _____.
   a. "those who serve"
   b. "Three Obediences"
   c. "loyalty to country"
   d. "way of the warrior"

3. After World War II, Japan no longer had _____.
   a. a samurai class
   b. an army
   c. large companies
   d. land owners

4. A play is performed in Japan about two brave samurai sisters who fought _____.
   a. for their independence
   b. to avenge their father's death
   c. against the emperor
   d. to preserve the samurai way of life

5. The samurai became very powerful in Japan around _____.
   a. the 1200s
   b. the early 1600s
   c. the Edo period
   d. 1867

6. The samurai lost their battle with the emperor because they _____.
   a. were no longer brave fighters
   b. had to hide in the hills
   c. didn't have modern weapons
   d. lost their leader, Saigo Takamori

7. When samurai were not fighting, they wore _____.
   a. clothing made from leather strips
   b. a piece of silk around their waist
   c. a suit of armor
   d. simple clothes

8. _____ is NOT part of the samurai code of ethics.
   a. Loyalty to the emperor or lord
   b. Generosity to the poor
   c. Trust in material wealth
   d. Kindness to others

MAKING INFERENCES

The answers to these questions are not directly stated in the article. Write complete sentences.

1. What kind of living area or home would a samurai likely have?

   _____

2. How do you think people reacted when they saw or met a samurai?

   _____

3. What can we infer about the rights of Japanese women between the 1600s and modern times?

   _____

4. What conclusions can you draw from the fact that the samurai helped to create several Japanese forms of art?

   _____

5. Why do you think the emperor abolished the samurai class?

   _____

6. Why couldn't some samurai survive after their status and privileges were taken away?

   _____

7. Why did the samurai rebels continue to fight even when they knew they had no chance of winning?

_____

8. What will probably happen to Bushido values in Japan?

_____

DISCUSSION

Discuss the answers to these questions with your classmates.

1. Do you think the samurai code of ethics is a good set of values to live by? Do you think there is a place for such a code in today's modern world? Why or why not?
2. What do you think of samurai women? Do you think women should carry weapons and know how to fight? Do you think women should fight on the battlefield with men?
3. Would you like to have been a samurai warrior? Why or why not?
4. If the emperor had not defeated the samurai, do you think they would still exist today? Why or why not?

WRITING

On separate paper, write a paragraph or an essay about one of the following topics:

1. Write arguments for and / or against women becoming part of the armed forces of a country.
2. What are two or three values or principles that you follow? (For example: being honest, working hard, respecting older people)
3. Which is more important for you, material things or honor and pride? Choose one and give reasons.

GRAMMAR AND PUNCTUATION

SEMICOLONS

1. **When there is no coordinating conjunction (*and, but, or, nor, so, yet*) between independent clauses in a sentence and the relationship is clear, we use a semicolon (;) to separate them.**

   They wore their hair tied back in a top-knot; their brow and crown were shaved.

2. **If the relationship between the independent clauses is not clear with a semicolon alone, we can use a transitional expression as well.**

   They knew they had no chance; nevertheless, they fought to the end.

Add semicolons to the following sentences where necessary.

1. When a samurai used a bow and arrow, he was an expert when he used a sword, he was a master.

2. In the beginning, samurai women were very independent after the 1600s, they had to follow the religious beliefs of that time.

3. Material things were not important for the samurai instead, honor and pride were important.

4. In the Edo period, Japan became a peaceful country its rulers didn't want the samurai to fight any more.

5. During this period, the samurai had a good life they lived in castles, were paid with rice, and had special rights.

6. Big companies in Japan are like families therefore, loyalty to one company is important.

7. The samurai don't exist in modern Japan their values live on, though.

8. Japan no longer has an army however, it has many huge companies.

9. The Samurai code was called *Bushido* this word means "way of the warrior."

10. The Samurai were interested in honor additionally, they had to be men of noble spirit.

UNIT 6

What Does Hair Tell Us About People?

BEFORE YOU READ

Answer these questions.

1. Do you like your current hairstyle? Why or why not?
2. What does a hairstyle say about a person?
3. If you could have any hairstyle, what would it be?

What Does Hair Tell Us About People?

1 Throughout history, hair has always been used to **make a fashion statement**. It also tells us a lot about culture. In almost all societies, people have cut or styled their hair for practical or decorative reasons. For example, the ancient Greeks liked blond hair, so both men and women lightened their hair. On the other hand, the Romans preferred dark hair, and Saxon men are seen in paintings to have hair and beards of blue, green, bright red, and orange. The Assyrian culture made an art of hairstyling. People curled, oiled, and perfumed their hair; they also cut their hair and beards in **layers** to look like pyramids. Assyrian soldiers needed to have their hair properly curled before they went to war. The Assyrian people used hairstyles to show their position and employment. Assyrian women of high rank, as well as women in Egypt, put on **fake** beards at meetings to show authority.

2 Hair is often a sign of superiority. Primitive men put bones, feathers, and other objects in their hair to impress and **intimidate** their enemies. Later, the Romans made the people they conquered cut off their hair to show submission. In seventeenth century China, Manchu men shaved the front of the hair and combed the hair in the back into a braided tail. They also made those they conquered wear this style.

3 Some cultures consider hair to be a **sensuous** object. For some people, not having hair or not showing it to others is a sign of religious devotion. Christian and Buddhist monks often shave their heads to show holiness and retirement from the world. Many Christian nuns cover their hair. Some Muslim women cover their hair when they are **in public**, and men in certain countries wear a turban or head cloth for religious reasons.

4 In ancient and modern times, hair has been used to **reveal** a person's emotions, **marital status**, or age. For example, ancient Egyptian men and women usually shaved their hair. However, when they were **in mourning**, they grew it long. Hindu women, on the other hand, cut off their long hair as a sign of mourning. In medieval Europe, unmarried women showed their long hair in public, whereas married women covered theirs. Today, brides in the Maasai tribe in Africa have their heads shaved as part of their marriage ceremony, and mothers in the tribe shave their sons' hair when the boys become adolescents. Today, teenagers all over the world **demonstrate** their youth and individuality through haircuts or hair colors. Even in countries like China and Japan,

where dyed hair is considered untraditional, up to 68 percent of women and 20 percent of men—most of them young—now use hair color to **reflect** their individual personalities.

5 Wigs have always been popular as fashion statements and as signs of wealth or status. Ancient Egyptians shaved their heads for cleanliness and then covered their heads with wigs. The higher the status of a person, the bigger his or her wig was. Cleopatra wore different styles and colors of wigs, and another Egyptian queen wore such a heavy wig on important occasions that attendants had to help her walk. Queen Elizabeth I of England wore a red wig because her own red hair was falling out, so all the rich men and women copied her and either dyed their hair red or wore red wigs. In France, King Louis XIV, who was also going bald, started the fashion of elaborate wigs. Naturally, everyone wanted to look like him, so they all started to wear wigs, too. At one time, forty wig makers were employed full-time just to make wigs for the people in the palace of Versailles!

6 These elaborate wig fashions went over to England, which always copied the French for style. Wigs became common for the middle and upper classes in England and France. They were powdered white because people thought this **flattered** the face and made their eyes look brighter. The fashion spread to divisions of the law, the army, and the navy, each of which had its own style of wig. However, by the end of the 1700s, hairstyles for women became extravagant to the point of **ridicule**. Rich women would spend hours with hairdressers who built tall wire cages on the women's heads. They covered the cages with hair and wigs and then greased the hair with fat so the white powder would stick to it. Finally, they decorated the hair with jewels, feathers, ornaments, and even flowers with water containers to keep them fresh. The women would wear their hair this way for two or three weeks. Obviously, they had to sleep in a sitting position at night and they could not wash their hair, but once a week they had to "open the hair" to get rid of the insects living in it. Fortunately, the French revolution in 1789 put an end to such extravagance, and hairstyles became simple again.

7 In the twentieth century, women in western cultures used their hair to show their growing independence. They often simplified their hairstyles to fit their busy lifestyles. For example, in the 1920s and 1930s, women cut their hair as **a symbol of** liberation. In the 1950s and 1960s, many women in the United States used wigs to **save time**. Instead of styling their hair every morning, they would wear a pre-styled wig. Some

women alternated between several wigs so that they could choose a style or color to match their clothes or even their mood!

8 Due to such changes, fashionable hairstyles no longer became **limited to** the rich—they were for everyone. And as the popularity of movies and television grew, women started to copy the hairstyles of famous stars, such as the short cut of Greta Garbo or the platinum blond hair color of Jean Harlow. More recently, thousands of American women **imitated** Jennifer Aniston's "Rachel" haircut seen on the popular TV show *Friends*. Men and boys also copy the hairstyles of movie or sports stars. In England, for example, boys often have their hair cut like the British soccer player David Beckham.

9 Today's hairstyles have become more relaxed and individual, so both men and women can choose a style that fits their life and expresses their personality. Whether they are rich or poor, people can choose the color or style of their hair—or even of a wig—to suit their own taste.

VOCABULARY

 MEANING

Circle the letter of the answer that is closest in meaning to the underlined word.

1. Assyrians cut their hair in <u>layers</u> to look like pyramids.
   a. unusual shapes
   b. different levels
   c. special ceremonies
   d. short styles

2. Today, teenagers <u>demonstrate</u> their youth and individuality through haircuts or hair colors.
   a. celebrate
   b. hide
   c. behave like
   d. show

3. Women <u>imitated</u> the haircut seen on a popular TV show.
   a. laughed at
   b. did the opposite of
   c. took parts of
   d. did the same as

4. Women in Egypt put on <u>fake</u> beards.
   a. not real
   b. colorful
   c. newly made
   d. natural

5. Hairstyles for women became extravagant to the point of <u>ridicule</u>.
   a. being made fun of
   b. getting respect for
   c. being famous for
   d. receiving praise for

6. Both women and men now use hair color to <u>reflect</u> their personalities.
   a. try to hide
   b. give a sign of
   c. try to change
   d. make better

7. Some cultures consider hair to be a <u>sensuous</u> object.
   a. having a certain style
   b. pleasing to the senses
   c. looking very unusual
   d. making a lot of trouble

8. Wigs were powdered white because people thought this <u>flattered</u> the face.
   a. made it smaller
   b. made it more pale
   c. made it more attractive
   d. made it look younger

9. Primitive men put objects in their hair to <u>intimidate</u> their enemies.
   a. kill
   b. harm
   c. defeat
   d. frighten

10. Hair has been used to <u>reveal</u> a person's emotions, marital status, or age.

    a. try to cover

    b. show respect for

    c. make known

    d. laugh at

 WORDS THAT GO TOGETHER

A. Find words in the reading that go together with the words below to make phrases.

1. limited _____

2. _____ public

3. _____ symbol _____

4. _____ mourning

5. marital _____

6. _____ a _____ statement

7. _____ time

B. Complete the sentences with the phrases from Part A.

1. When you are _____, you feel very sad because someone special to you has died.

2. To do something more quickly is to _____.

3. To be in an area among other people is to be _____.

4. When something is _____ one group or a place, it happens only in that group or area.

5. The state of being married or unmarried is a person's _____.

6. A sign or object that represents a person, thing, or idea is _____ it.

7. If you dress in a certain way in order to say something about yourself, you _____.

C. Now use the phrases in your own sentences.

Example: *I took a plane instead of driving because I wanted to* save time.

USE

Work with a partner to answer the questions. Use complete sentences.

1. What are three annoying things that some people do *in public*?
2. How do people in your culture show that they are *in mourning*?
3. What is an object or fashion that is *a symbol of* something else? Explain what it means.
4. What are two things that people wear that are often *fake*?
5. How do people use their clothing to *reveal* their emotions? Describe two ways.
6. Do you like to *make a fashion statement* with your clothing or hair? Explain.
7. Have you ever *imitated* a famous person's hairstyle or clothing? Describe what you did.
8. What modern fashions *demonstrate* the feelings or beliefs of today's teenagers?

COMPREHENSION

UNDERSTANDING MAIN IDEAS

Look at the reading to find the answers to the following questions.

1. What is the main idea of paragraph 1?

   _____

2. Which sentence contains the main idea of paragraph 4?

   _____

3. Which sentence states the main idea of paragraph 7?

   _____

4. What place have wigs had in the history of hair?

   _____

5. What part did the popularity of movies and television play in the history of hair?

   _____

REMEMBERING DETAILS

Reread the passage and fill in the blanks.

1. In England and France, wigs were powdered white because

   _____.

2. In Africa, brides in the Maasai tribe have their heads shaved as part of their _____.

3. A recent popular hairstyle was _____,
   which an actress had on the TV show *Friends*.

4. During the reign of Queen Elizabeth I, the rich men and women of England dyed their hair _____.

5. Before Assyrian soldiers went to war, they _____.

6. In the 1920s and 1930s, women cut their hair as a symbol of

   _____.

7. Christian and Buddhist monks often shave their heads to show

   _____.

8. In the late 1700s, women had to "open the hair" of their elaborate hairstyles in order to _____.

MAKING INFERENCES

The answers to these questions can be inferred, or guessed, from the reading. Circle the letter of the best answer.

1. The reading implies that in the past _____.
   a. wealth had little to do with how people wore their hair
   b. the wealthy usually had more simple hairstyles than the common people
   c. royalty often started new fashions in hair
   d. people with wealth and status did not consider hairstyles important

2. It can be inferred from the reading that _____.
   a. the only purpose of hair styling has been to make people more beautiful
   b. hair styling has only been popular in modern times
   c. only advanced cultures have been interested in styling their hair
   d. people have always styled their hair for more reasons than beauty

3. From the reading, it can be concluded that _____.
   a. ideas about style and beauty have not changed much over time
   b. we can learn a lot about a culture from the hairstyles of its people
   c. hair styling is not as important today as it was in the past
   d. hairstyles tell us very little about society in general

4. The reading implies that in the 1700s, hairstyles _____.
   a. were not important
   b. were only for women
   c. were ridiculously elaborate
   d. had nothing to do with beauty

5. It can be inferred from the reading that in ancient times, hairstyles _____.
   a. were a symbol of power
   b. were the same in most cultures
   c. were used only for practical reasons
   d. were very simple

DISCUSSION

Discuss the answers to these questions with your classmates.

1. How have hairstyles changed for men and women in your country over the last hundred years?
2. Describe the current hairstyles in your country for men, women, children, and older adults. What do these hairstyles say about your culture?
3. Why do you think every new generation likes to wear a different hairstyle from what their parents wore?
4. What are some common influences on people's choices of clothes and hairstyles today? What are some of the things that influence you?

WRITING

On separate paper, write a paragraph or an essay about one of the following topics:

1. What are the two factors that can influence young people's choice of hairstyle or clothes?
2. What hairstyles or clothes are or have been extreme to the point of ridicule? Explain.
3. What styles are or have reflected economic or social changes?

GRAMMAR AND PUNCTUATION

COMMAS: AFTER INTRODUCTORY WORDS AND PHRASES

> **We usually use a comma to set off introductory words or phrases at the beginning of a sentence. The comma shows that we pause after we say these words. Remember that a phrase does not have a subject and a verb.**
>
> *Throughout history,* hair has always made a fashion statement.
>
> *In almost all societies,* people have cut or styled their hair.
>
> *Finally,* they decorated the hair with jewels, feathers, and ornaments.

Add commas to the following sentences where necessary.

1. As the popularity of movies grew men and women copied the hairstyles of movie stars.
2. A few years ago young women copied the hairstyle of Jennifer Aniston, who appeared in the TV show *Friends*.
3. Today's hairstyles express people's personalities.
4. In ancient Egypt women shaved their heads for cleanliness.
5. In some parts of the world hair can reveal marital status, age, or even emotion.
6. At one time all the middle- and upper-class men and women in England wore wigs.
7. Women of high rank in ancient Egypt wore fake beards.
8. By cutting their hair short women showed their liberation.
9. He colored his hair to look younger.
10. In time wigs that were very elaborate went out of fashion.

UNIT 7

How Did Chopsticks Originate?

BEFORE YOU READ

Answer these questions.

1. In which countries do people use chopsticks?
2. How long have people used chopsticks?
3. Do you ever eat with chopsticks?

How Did Chopstick Originate?

1 In the beginning, people used just their fingers to eat. Then came the finger-and-knife combination. Around 5,000 years ago, while the rest of the world was still using fingers and a knife, the Chinese began using chopsticks. Today many people eat with a combination of knives, spoons, and forks, but chopsticks are still as important and popular as they were centuries ago.

2 No one knows exactly when the Chinese began to use chopsticks. **According to** one Chinese legend, the use of chopsticks began when two poor farmers were **thrown out** of their village. The farmers went from village to village, but were not welcome anywhere. The two men grew tired and hungry, so they stole a piece of meat from a storeroom in a small village. Then they ran from the village and into a forest, where they quickly made a fire to cook their meat. The smell of the roasting meat was so good that the two men could not wait any longer. Using some sticks from the forest floor, they took the pieces of meat from the fire and put them into their mouths. And so began the popularity of chopsticks. Other people did the same, and in a short time people all over China were eating with chopsticks.

3 There are other ideas about why the Chinese started using chopsticks. Some people believe that the philosopher Confucius influenced how the Chinese thought about many things, including how they ate. Confucius, a vegetarian, said it was wrong to have knives at the table because knives were used for killing. Another idea is that there was not enough **fuel** in China. There was only a small amount of fuel available for the cooking of food. But the Chinese **found the solution**! They cut up the food into small pieces before cooking, so it would cook as quickly as possible and only use a very small amount of fuel. The small pieces of food were well suited for chopsticks. It is not certain which came first: chopsticks or the **unique** style of Chinese cooking. But it is certain that chopsticks did have a great influence on the development of Chinese cooking.

4 Chopsticks spread from China to Vietnam and Korea and **eventually** reached Japan by the year 500. Over 3,000 years and between different cultures, several **variations** of chopsticks developed. Chinese chopsticks are nine to ten inches long and round or square at the top end. The Vietnamese did not change the Chinese chopsticks, but the Koreans made their chopsticks a little thinner and then started to make them from

metal. Korea is the only country today that uses metal chopsticks. The Japanese made their chopsticks rounded and pointed. They are also shorter—seven inches long for females and eight inches long for males.

5 Every kind of material is used to make chopsticks. The vast majority of chopsticks are made from bamboo. Bamboo is cheap, **heat resistant**, and has no taste or **odor**. The wealthy have had chopsticks made from gold, jade, ivory, and silver. Some people had strong feelings about some of these materials. In fact, people once believed silver chopsticks would turn black if they touched any poison. An emperor who was afraid of being poisoned made his servants test each of the dishes with silver chopsticks before he ate. The emperor himself would not use silver chopsticks to eat; he thought the metal in his mouth was unpleasant. Today we know that silver doesn't **react to** poisons, but if bad eggs, onions, or garlic are used, the chemicals might change the color of silver chopsticks.

6 The Japanese made chopsticks from every kind of tree. They even started to put lacquer, a kind of shiny paint, on chopsticks about 400 years ago. The lacquered chopsticks of modern Japan have designs and are beautiful to look at. They are given as special gifts because they are not only beautiful, but **durable**. The layers of lacquer make them last **forever**. The Wajima Nuri area in Japan is famous for making chopsticks with between 75 and 120 separate layers of lacquer. These chopsticks are harder than metal and can cost up to $125 a pair.

7 In 1878, the Japanese were also the first to make **disposable** wooden chopsticks. The disposable chopstick started when a Japanese schoolteacher named Tadao Shimamoto had packed his lunch and brought it to school with him but had **left behind** his pair of chopsticks. Fortunately, his school was in an area of Japan famous for its wood. He explained his problem to one of the local men. The man gave him a piece of wood from which Tadao made a pair of chopsticks. Anyone who has eaten in a Japanese or Chinese restaurant knows what these look like. People liked his chopsticks so much that soon the local area started to produce large numbers of disposable chopsticks called *wari-bashi*. We do not know if Tadao made any money from wari-bashi, but certainly his name is remembered. Each year representatives from disposable chopstick manufacturers go to Tadao's **hometown** and perform a ceremony **in honor of** the father of wari-bashi.

8 About one-half of disposable chopsticks are produced in Japan; the rest come from China, Indonesia, Korea, and the Philippines. Japan uses about 24 billion pairs of disposable chopsticks a year, which is a lot of wood. In fact, it is enough to build over 10,000 homes. Japan now is trying to **eliminate** them for environmental reasons. Today, increasing numbers of Japanese are trying to help the environment. They carry their own personal chopsticks to restaurants instead of using disposable ones. But no matter what kind of chopsticks people use, chopsticks are here to stay.

VOCABULARY

MEANING

Circle the letter of the answer that is closest in meaning to the underlined word.

1. Chopsticks <u>eventually</u> reached Japan by the year 500.
   a. in the course of time   c. at an earlier time
   b. in a short time   d. at the right time

2. In 1878, the Japanese were the first to make <u>disposable</u> wooden chopsticks.
   a. made to be used many times   c. made to be used in a restaurant
   b. made to be folded and put away d. made to be used once and thrown away

3. Japan now is trying to <u>eliminate</u> disposable chopsticks for environmental reasons.
   a. increase the number of   c. limit the use of
   b. get rid of   d. make copies of

4. It is not certain which came first: chopsticks or the <u>unique</u> style of Chinese cooking.
   a. like many others   c. unlike any other
   b. very old and traditional   d. not as good as others

5. Lacquered chopsticks are given as special gifts because they are not only beautiful, but also <u>durable</u>.
   a. heavy   c. delicate
   b. lasting   d. elegant

6. There was not enough <u>fuel</u> in China.
   a. equipment that is used during the cooking process
   b. tools that are used to eat meals
   c. material that is burned to produce heat or power
   d. wood that is used to carve bowls and spoons

7. Bamboo has no taste or <u>odor</u>.
   a. smell
   b. shape
   c. color
   d. strength

8. Representatives go to Tadao's <u>hometown</u> and perform a ceremony.
   a. place where he grew up
   b. place where he worked
   c. place where he died
   d. place where he went to school

9. The layers of lacquer make them last <u>forever</u>.
   a. for a short while
   b. for a long while
   c. for one time
   d. for all time

10. Several <u>variations</u> of chopsticks developed.
    a. parts
    b. imitations
    c. uses
    d. different types

WORDS THAT GO TOGETHER

A. **Find words in the reading that go together with the words below to make phrases.**

1. left _____
2. react _____
3. thrown _____
4. _____ honor _____
5. _____ resistant
6. according _____
7. _____ the solution

B. **Complete the sentences with the phrases from Part A.**

1. When someone is _____ of a place, he is forced to leave because of bad behavior.

2. _____ means "as said by someone" or "as shown by something."

3. To _____ something means to experience a change when coming in contact with it.

4. If you _____, you figured out the answer to a problem.

5. If someone _____ something, they forgot to bring it.

6. To do something _____ someone is to show respect for that person.

7. If something is _____, it will not get hot, even when it gets near a fire or other source of heat.

C. Now use the phrases in your own sentences.

Example: According to *the weather service, it's going to rain tomorrow.*

USE

Work with a partner to answer the questions. Use complete sentences.

1. What kind of food has a strong *odor*?
2. What kind of *fuel* is used to cook in your home?
3. What are two *variations* in how your favorite food is cooked?
4. What are two types of materials that are very *durable*?
5. Where is your *hometown*? Describe it.
6. What do you use that is *disposable*?
7. What experience have you had that you wish would last *forever*?
8. Where are some places that someone might be *thrown out* of for bad behavior?

COMPREHENSION

UNDERSTANDING MAIN IDEAS

Look at the reading to find the answers to the following questions.

1. Which sentence contains the main idea of paragraph 2?

   _____

2. Which sentence states the main idea of paragraph 4?

   _____

3. What is the main idea of paragraph 7?

   _____

4. How did chopsticks solve a problem in China?

   _____

5. Why have disposable chopsticks become a problem in Japan?

   _____

REMEMBERING DETAILS

Reread the passage and circle the letter of the best answer.

1. Japanese chopsticks are _____.
   a. nine to ten inches long   c. the same as Chinese chopsticks
   b. thin and made of metal   d. rounded and pointed

2. Disposable chopsticks were first made by _____.
   a. a Japanese schoolteacher   c. Confucius
   b. two poor Chinese farmers   d. the Koreans

3. Chopsticks are NOT made from _____.
   a. metal   c. bamboo
   b. paper   d. jade

4. The Chinese began using chopsticks _____.
   a. in the year 500   c. around 5,000 years ago
   b. about 3,000 years ago   d. in 1878

5. The emperor would not use silver chopsticks because he _____.
   a. thought they would poison   c. only wanted chopsticks made
      his food   from gold
   b. thought they would turn his   d. didn't like the metal taste
      tongue black

6. The Japanese give as gifts beautiful chopsticks made with many layers of
_____.

    a. bamboo   c. metal
    b. lacquer   d. ivory

7. In the Chinese style of cooking, food is _____ before it is cooked.

    a. cut into small pieces   c. placed on an open fire
    b. tested for poison   d. mixed with onions and garlic

8. Confucius was a Chinese _____.

    a. schoolteacher   c. emperor
    b. cook   d. philosopher

MAKING INFERENCES

Some of the following statements are facts from the reading. Other statements can be inferred, or guessed. Write *F* for each factual statement. Write *I* for each inference.

_____ 1. When two poor farmers used sticks to pick up hot meat, they had no idea that they were starting a new method of eating in China.

_____ 2. Confucius was a vegetarian, and he said it was wrong to have knives at the table because knives were used for killing.

_____ 3. Chopsticks are not suitable for eating all types of food.

_____ 4. Chopsticks are made from many different types of materials.

_____ 5. People believed that silver chopsticks would turn black if they touched poison, but today we know that isn't true.

_____ 6. The most famous area in Japan for making lacquered chopsticks is Wajima Nuri.

_____ 7. Tadao Shimamoto wasn't trying to create a new product for sale when he made his first pair of disposable chopsticks.

_____ 8. Disposable chopsticks are very useful to people but are not so good for the world in which we live.

_____ 9. Chopsticks don't work very well for cutting or picking up large pieces of food.

_____10. In Japan, men and women use different lengths of chopsticks.

DISCUSSION

Discuss the answers to these questions with your classmates.

1. Today, we use a lot of disposable things that are bad for the environment. Should we stop using some disposable items? Which ones?
2. What are some dos and don'ts for eating at the table in your country?
3. What are the advantages and / or disadvantages of these three ways of eating: with fingers; with fork, knife, and spoon; with chopsticks? Which do you prefer? Why?
4. What steps can we take to protect our environment?

WRITING

On separate paper, write a paragraph or an essay about one of the following topics:

1. What are the advantages and / or disadvantages of using disposable products?
2. Describe how you usually serve and eat food in your country.
3. What are the advantages and / or disadvantages of eating fast foods?

GRAMMAR AND PUNCTUATION

 HYPHENS

We use a hyphen (-) to form compound words (words made by combining two or more words) and to join prefixes and suffixes to root words.

(Note: The use of the hyphen in compound words changes over time. As a compound word becomes more common, we stop hyphenating it. It is always a good idea to check in a dictionary if you are not sure.)

We usually use a hyphen:

- for fractions and compound numbers from twenty-one to ninety-nine

   one-half *of the chopsticks*   **seventy-five** *layers of lacquer*

- with the prefixes *all-, ex-,* and *self-*

   all-*powerful*   **ex-***president*   **self-***service*

- with all prefixes before a proper noun or a proper adjective

   post-*World War II*   **pro-***Japanese*

> - to connect certain compound nouns
>
>   **stir-fry**   **good-bye**
>
> - to connect compound adjectives that come before a noun
>
>   a **heat-resistant** wood   an **old-fashioned** restaurant

A. Correct the errors in hyphen use. Add hyphens where necessary.

1. one third of grown ups

    _____

2. one-hundred and twenty five million

    _____

3. a left handed-person

    _____

4. bite sized pieces

    _____

5. hand polished chopsticks

    _____

6. anti disposable chopstick campaign

    _____

B. Find and correct the errors in hyphen use. Then compare answers with a partner.

    Koreans love short grain sticky rice. There is always some rice that sticks to the bottom of the cooking pot. When Koreans serve dinner, they add enough water to cover the stuck on rice (about three fourths of a cup). They leave this to cook through the dinner. After dinner, the rice water tea is drunk in the same way as the Western after dinner coffee.

UNIT 8

Where Did Certain Wedding Customs Come From?

BEFORE YOU READ

Answer these questions.

1. Do you like to attend weddings? Why or why not?
2. What are some wedding customs in your country?
3. Do you prefer a traditional or modern wedding? Why?

Where Did Certain Wedding Customs Come From?

1 Everywhere around the world, weddings are celebrated with some kind of ceremony. These ceremonies differ between cultures, but many of the customs **associated with** wedding ceremonies—such as the wedding ring, the wedding dress, the wedding cake, and throwing confetti—come from common beliefs and similar ancient traditions.

2 The idea of the wedding ring started with the ancient Hindus. It was not considered to be a symbol of love in the beginning. It was, in fact, a sign that a **down payment** had been given for the woman and that she was no longer **available**. In some tribes in Africa, women are still bought. In 1964, a chief of the Maasai tribe offered 150 cows, 20 goats, and $750 cash to buy American actress Carroll Baker. This was a lot, **considering** the best Maasai fighter then paid $200 and 12 cows for a wife!

3 The ancient Greeks and Romans took the idea of wedding rings from the Hindus, and they also kept the ring as a sign that a young lady was "sold." Christian societies **adopted** the ring around the year 1000 as a sign of **fidelity**. The ring, a circle with no beginning and no end, also was a symbol of **eternity**. The Scandinavians did not adopt the custom of wedding rings until the late 1600s. Before then, they preferred to break a gold or silver coin and have each partner keep one-half.

4 There are also various beliefs about which hand and finger to put the ring on. The ancient Greeks and Romans wore the ring on the fourth finger of the left hand because they believed that a **vein** ran directly to the heart from that finger. However, wedding rings are not worn on the left hand in every country. In Chile and Germany, couples exchange rings when they get engaged, wear their rings on their left hand until they are married, and then **switch** them to their right hands. In Russia, there is no special finger for a wedding ring. However, people there usually wear a ring on the right hand to **indicate** they have a partner. In some countries, like Brazil, couples wear rings on the left hand and have their names inscribed inside the ring: the bride has the groom's name in her ring and **vice versa**. In Sweden, women wear three rings: one for engagement, one for marriage, and one for motherhood.

5 Today many brides marry in a white dress, which symbolizes purity. This tradition started in the 1500s. Before that time, brides wore their

best dress, and the color **did not matter**. Today, in the United States and Britain, brides wear white dresses and follow the tradition of wearing, "something old, something new, something borrowed, something blue." Each "something" has a special meaning. "Something old" is a symbol of past happiness and symbolizes the transfer of these feelings to the bride's marriage. "Something new" symbolizes the hoped-for success of the marriage, and it often takes the form of a new dress. "Something borrowed" represents the hope that the loyalty of friends will continue through the marriage, and "something blue" stands for fidelity, since blue is the color that symbolizes this value. In Japan, white was always the color for a bride even before it became popular in Western cultures. A Japanese bride may sometimes change her dress two or three times on her wedding day. She may start with a traditional kimono and end with a Western-style white dress. In Finland, brides wear white dresses and golden crowns. After the wedding ceremony, guests cover the bride's eyes, and the unmarried women dance around her as she puts the crown on one of their heads. Whoever she crowns, it is believed, will be the next bride.

6 White is not the color worn by brides everywhere. In China and Pakistan, brides wear red, which symbolizes happiness. In Samoa, brides wear a dress made of material from the bark of a tree, along with fresh flowers and a crown of mother of pearl. In the past, it was **common practice** in many cultures for the bride and the bridesmaids to wear the same color as a way of confusing evil spirits that might hurt the bride. Today, this tradition is still present in the Philippines.

7 The idea of the wedding cake is common throughout the world. Originally, the wedding cake was not eaten by the bride. It was thrown at her! People thought that throwing cake at a bride would bring her **fertility**. It originally started with throwing wheat, which later took the form of little cakes. Later, the cakes were **piled** on top of each other, and a higher pile meant more prosperity for the couple. Finally, a French chef thought of the multi-layered cake that is common in Western cultures today. Many countries have their own traditional cakes: the Irish have a fruitcake, in the Ukraine it is a wedding bread, in Denmark it is an almond cake with beautifully decorated sugar work, and in France they have caramel-coated cream puffs.

8 Throwing things at the couple to wish them fertility or prosperity is also common throughout different cultures. People in the United States traditionally threw rice at couples as they left the place where they got married. When people learned that the rice was making birds sick, they

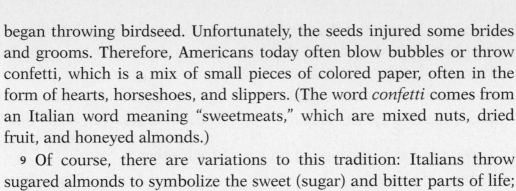

began throwing birdseed. Unfortunately, the seeds injured some brides and grooms. Therefore, Americans today often blow bubbles or throw confetti, which is a mix of small pieces of colored paper, often in the form of hearts, horseshoes, and slippers. (The word *confetti* comes from an Italian word meaning "sweetmeats," which are mixed nuts, dried fruit, and honeyed almonds.)

9 Of course, there are variations to this tradition: Italians throw sugared almonds to symbolize the sweet (sugar) and bitter parts of life; in the Czech Republic, people throw peas; in Romania, it's sweets and nuts. Throwing shoes once was preferred over throwing wheat, rice, or birdseed, because in the old days people believed shoes were a symbol of fertility. The Inuit of North America still have this tradition. It is also common today in the United States and Britain to tie shoes to the back of the newlyweds' car.

10 Even in our modern traditions, we still use ancient symbols to show our wishes for marriage unions to be happy and fruitful. Most of these wedding customs from around the world have things **in common** and come from shared human values. Though many customs are based on ancient traditions and superstitions that we may not **be aware of** today, they have the same purpose: They all celebrate marriage and wish the new couple well.

VOCABULARY

 MEANING

Circle the letter of the answer that is closest in meaning to the underlined word.

1. People thought that throwing cake at a bride would bring her <u>fertility</u>.
   a. the talent to make money
   b. the good health to live a long life
   c. the ability to have babies
   d. the faithfulness to have a good marriage

2. Christian societies <u>adopted</u> the ring around the year 1000.
   a. began to use or have
   b. put aside
   c. refused to accept
   d. changed according to their wishes

3. Ancient Greeks and Romans wore the ring on the fourth finger of the left hand because they believed that a <u>vein</u> ran directly to the heart from that finger.
   a. a nerve that sends signals
   b. a tube that carries blood
   c. a muscle that makes movement
   d. an organ that beats quickly

4. Later, the cakes were <u>piled</u> on top of each other.
   a. put side by side
   b. covered by something
   c. placed one on the other
   d. separated into groups

5. This was a lot, <u>considering</u> the best Maasai fighter paid $200 and 12 cows for a wife.
   a. comparing
   b. wondering about
   c. forgetting about
   d. keeping in mind

6. People in Russia usually wear a ring on the right hand to <u>indicate</u> they have a partner.
   a. design
   b. describe
   c. show
   d. remind

7. It was a sign that the woman was no longer <u>available</u>.
   a. free to begin a romance
   b. attractive to other men
   c. young enough for marriage
   d. valuable to own

8. Christian societies adopted the ring as a sign of <u>fidelity</u>.
   a. faithfulness
   b. love
   c. friendship
   d. good fortune

9. The ring was also was a symbol of <u>eternity</u>.
   a. a number of years
   b. the present time
   c. time without end
   d. a moment

10. After they are married, they <u>switch</u> their rings to their right hands.
    a. take off
    b. change
    c. turn over
    d. hold

WORDS THAT GO TOGETHER

A. Find words in the reading that go together with the words below to make phrases.

1. _____ practice
2. _____ payment
3. _____ versa
4. associated _____
5. _____ aware _____
6. _____ common
7. _____ matter

B. Complete the sentences with the phrases from Part A.

1. When people or things share something, such as a quality or interest, they are thought to have it _____.
2. _____ means "in the opposite way."
3. When something _____, it was not important.
4. Something that is done often by many people is _____.
5. Things that are related, or connected, are _____ each other.
6. When you pay part of the price for something in order to hold it as your future possession, you are giving a _____ for that property.
7. To _____ something is to have knowledge or understanding of it.

C. Now use the phrases in your own sentences.

Example: *It is* common practice *in my company to reward good workers.*

USE

Work with a partner to answer the questions. Use complete sentences.

1. What are two kinds of purchases that often require a *down payment*?
2. What does *fidelity* between two people mean?
3. What are two items that are made of things *piled* on each other?
4. What is a holiday custom that is *common practice* in your culture?
5. What famous person would you like to *switch* lives with?

6. How can someone with a partner or spouse show that he or she is no longer *available*?

7. What kinds of celebrations do most societies have *in common*?

8. What is a custom that your culture has *adopted* from another culture?

COMPREHENSION

UNDERSTANDING MAIN IDEAS

Some of the following statements are main ideas, and some are supporting statements. Some of them are stated directly in the reading. Find the statements. Write *M* for each main idea. Write *S* for each supporting statement.

_____ 1. In Sweden, women wear three rings: one for engagement, one for marriage, and one for motherhood.

_____ 2. Today many brides marry in a white dress, which symbolizes purity.

_____ 3. The idea of the wedding cake is common throughout the world.

_____ 4. "Something borrowed" represents the hope that the loyalty of friends will continue through the marriage.

_____ 5. There are also various beliefs about which hand and finger to put the ring on.

_____ 6. It is also common today in the United States and Britain to tie shoes to the back of the newlyweds' car.

REMEMBERING DETAILS

Reread the passage and circle the letter of the best answer.

1. The multi-layered cake that is common in Western cultures today was first created by _____.
   a. an American bride
   b. a man in the Ukraine
   c. a French chef
   d. a baker in Denmark

2. In the old days, people believed shoes were a symbol of _____.
   a. prosperity
   b. faithfulness
   c. happiness
   d. fertility

3. The idea of the wedding ring started with the ancient _____.
   a. Greeks   c. African tribes
   b. Romans   d. Hindus

4. The Japanese bride may start her wedding day by wearing a _____.
   a. traditional kimono   c. white dress and golden crown
   b. Western-style white dress   d. red dress

5. In many cultures in the past, the bride and bridesmaids wore the same colors in order to _____.
   a. play tricks on the groom   c. bring the bride fertility
   b. confuse evil spirits   d. show the faithfulness of friends

6. In Brazil, engaged couples wear rings _____.
   a. inscribed with each other's names   c. on no special finger
   b. on their right hands   d. in groups of three

7. In the Czech Republic, people throw _____ at the new couple.
   a. sugared almonds   c. peas
   b. sweets and nuts   d. rice

8. In the Ukraine, the traditional wedding cake is _____.
   a. an almond cake   c. a multi-layered cake
   b. caramel-coated cream puffs   d. a bread

MAKING INFERENCES

Some of the following statements can be inferred, or guessed, from the reading and others cannot. Circle the number of each statement that can be inferred.

1. Although the wearing of the wedding ring differs among cultures, the meaning of the ring is similar.
2. The use of the wedding ring is a fairly modern custom.
3. It has always been considered wrong among most cultures to think of a bride as property.
4. Most wedding ceremonies combine traditional and modern customs.
5. The color of a bride's dress is not important in most cultures.
6. Many wedding customs are related to the desire for a new couple to have children.

7. The wedding cake can take many forms.

8. The idea of throwing things at a couple is not very popular today.

DISCUSSION

Discuss the answers to these questions with your classmates.

1. Some people get married, but do not have a wedding celebration. Which way do you prefer? Why?

2. Besides a ring, what are some other symbols of love in today's world?

3. Why are wedding ceremonies and customs important to a couple? What purpose do they serve?

4. If you were getting married, what kind of wedding would you like to have?

WRITING

On separate paper, write a paragraph or an essay about one of the following topics:

1. Describe the three or four steps before a wedding takes place in your country.

2. Describe in three or four steps the wedding ceremony in your country.

3. Describe the traditional wedding dress, ring, and cake in your country.

GRAMMAR AND PUNCTUATION

COMMAS: TO SEPARATE INTERRUPTERS

Interrupters are expressions that create a pause in the flow of the sentence. We separate interrupters from the rest of the sentence by putting commas before and / or after them. These are some common interrupters:

after all	by the way	I believe	indeed
as we all know	for example	I think	naturally
as far as we know	however	in fact	of course

In fact, the wedding ring was a sign that a down payment had been given for the bride.

Whoever she crowns, it is believed, will be the next bride.

There are variations to this tradition, of course.

Add commas to the following sentences where necessary.

1. Most brides in Western cultures, as we all know wear white.
2. White however is not the color worn by brides everywhere.
3. As far as we know the idea of a wedding ring started with the ancient Hindus.
4. In Chile for example, couples wear wedding rings on their right hands.
5. Swedish women wear three rings by the way.
6. The girl who catches the bridal bouquet it is believed will be the next bride.
7. Naturally when people threw rice at the couple, some brides and grooms got injured.
8. Shoes are still used as a symbol of fertility by the Inuit of North America for example.
9. Indeed many of our wedding customs are based on ancient traditions and superstitions.
10. The purpose of all these customs after all is to wish the new couple well.

SELF-TEST 1
Units 1–8

A. SENTENCE COMPLETION

Circle the letter of the correct answer.

1. The stories of King Arthur _____ an age of heroism and romance.
   a. make think of
   b. makes we think of
   c. makes us think of
   d. make us think of

2. Inca rule was _____.
   a. organized and controlled
   b. organized and control
   c. organize and control
   d. organized and controls

3. Diwali lasts for five days and is one of _____ festivals for Hindus.
   a. the longer
   b. the longest
   c. longest
   d. the most longest

4. _____ stories of *The 1,001 Arabian Nights* is the story of Sherezade.
   a. The frame for
   b. The frame for the
   c. Frame for the
   d. The frames for the

5. The samurai warriors _____ by lords to fight their wars and protect their lands.
   a. were hired
   b. were hiring
   c. was hired
   d. were to hire

6. Throughout history, _____ told us a lot about people and culture.
   a. hair always
   b. hair have always
   c. hairs have always
   d. hair has always

7. Every kind of _____ to make chopsticks.
   a. materials is used
   b. materials are used
   c. materials used
   d. material is used

8. _____ with some kind of ceremony.
   a. Weddings are celebrated
   b. Weddings are celebrate
   c. Weddings celebrated
   d. Weddings celebrate

B. VOCABULARY

Complete the sentences. Circle the letter of the correct answer.

1. King Arthur was a character who _____ hundreds of stories.
   a. betrayed
   b. inspired
   c. allowed
   d. passed down

2. The Incas had a(n) _____ system of roads.
   a. inferior
   b. sophisticated
   c. industrialized
   d. piled

3. In India, Diwali is a time when light _____ over darkness.
   a. implores
   b. honors
   c. triumphs
   d. rejoices

4. *The 1,001 Arabian Nights* _____ what life was like in those times.
   a. depicts
   b. imitates
   c. encounters
   d. intimidates

5. The fighting skills of the samurai are the _____ martial arts today.
   a. rows of
   b. symbol of
   c. basis of
   d. combination of

6. At one time, hairstyles became extravagant to the point of _____.
   a. status
   b. privileges
   c. ridicule
   d. prosperity

7. Today, Japan is trying to _____ the use of disposable chopsticks for environmental reasons.
   a. neglect
   b. demonstrate
   c. eliminate
   d. switch

8. Christians used the wedding ring as a sign of _____.
   a. fidelity   c. significance
   b. attitude   d. reluctance

c. GRAMMAR AND PUNCTUATION

Circle the letter of the sentence or sentences with the correct grammar and punctuation.

1. a. King Arthur, together with his knights, were brave and fought for justice.
   b. King Arthur, together with his knights, was brave and fought for justice.
   c. King Arthur and his knights was brave and fought for justice.
   d. The knights of King Arthur was brave and fought for justice.

2. a. The Incas had huge storehouses all over the country. Therefore no one starved.
   b. The Incas had huge storehouses all over the country. No one, therefore starved.
   c. The Incas had huge storehouses all over the country. Therefore, no one starved.
   d. The Incas had huge storehouses all over the country. No one starved therefore.

3. a. Diwali she said is a time to be happy and enjoy family and friends.
   b. "Diwali," she said, "is a time to be happy and enjoy family and friends."
   c. Diwali she said "is a time to be happy and enjoy family and friends."
   d. "Diwali she said is a time to be happy and enjoy family and friends."

4. a. While the dazzled king listened, Sherezade stopped at the most exciting part of the story.
   b. While the dazzling king listened, Sherezade stopped at the most exciting part of the story.
   c. While the dazzled king listened, Sherezade stopped at the most excited part of the story.
   d. While the dazzling king listened, Sherezade stopping at the most excited part of the story.

5. a. In modern Japan, there are no more samurai, however, their values live on.
   b. In modern Japan, there are no more samurai; But their values live on.
   c. In modern Japan, there are no more samurai; however, their values live on.
   d. In modern Japan, there are no more samurai; their values live on.

6. a. In ancient Egypt, men and women shaved their heads for cleanliness.
   b. In ancient Egypt men and women shaved their heads for cleanliness.
   c. In ancient Egypt men and women, shaved their heads for cleanliness.
   d. In ancient Egypt men and women shaved their heads, for cleanliness.

7. a. In many Asian countries, food is cut into bite-size pieces and stir-fried.
   b. In many Asian countries, food is cut into bitesize pieces and stir-fried.
   c. In many Asian countries, food is cut into bite size pieces and stirfried.
   d. In many Asian countries, food is cut into bite-size pieces and stir fried.

8. a. Most wedding customs in fact are based on ancient traditions and superstitions.
   b. Most wedding customs, in fact are based on ancient traditions and superstitions.
   c. Most wedding customs, in fact, are based on ancient traditions and superstitions.
   d. In fact most wedding customs are based on ancient traditions and superstitions.

UNIT 9

Who Are the CyberAngels?

BEFORE YOU READ

Answer these questions.

1. Do you like working on a computer? Why or why not?
2. What are some problems you have when you use a computer?
3. What are some types of computer crimes?

Who Are the CyberAngels?

1 You are on the Internet **checking your e-mail**. There is a file attached to one of the messages, so you open it. After that, you start having problems with your computer. It starts very slowly, or it won't start **at all**. The names of your computer files start changing. Then you start getting calls from your friends—they are receiving e-mails from you that you never sent. Your computer probably received a virus through the e-mail attachment. Viruses are unsafe programs that **sneak into** and sometimes ruin computers. Some viruses can even find private information on your computer and deliver it to dishonest people. Now there is an organization that protects people from viruses and other types of Internet crime: It is called CyberAngels.

2 CyberAngels is part of Guardian Angels, a **volunteer organization** that makes the world safer for us to live in. But Guardian Angels didn't originally protect people from Internet crimes. It began before most people even had computers. The organization started in 1979 with Curtis Sliwa. At the time, Sliwa was the night manager at a McDonald's in a dangerous part of New York City. With his workers, he started the "Rock Brigade." The Brigade started to improve the **deteriorated** neighborhood by planting trees, cleaning up vacant lots, sweeping the sidewalks, and in general making the area more beautiful. The Rock Brigade got awards from the community and government groups.

3 The neighborhood was cleaned up, but the streets were not safer. At that time in New York, crime had increased, but the city had no money to **hire** police to control the crime. Older people would come to McDonald's because Sliwa would walk them home safely. One day, a retired **transit** worker begged him to do something about the street **muggers**. At this point, Sliwa decided to expand his clean-up program to include patrolling the subway. From his workers, he put together a multiracial group of volunteers. In the beginning, there were twelve volunteers, and together with Sliwa they were known as the "Magnificent Thirteen." Without weapons, they would walk the streets and **ride the subway** in the most dangerous areas to find the gang members who had been robbing people. Then they would hold these criminals until the police came to arrest them. They gradually took back the neighborhood; it was no longer **infested with** crime.

4 Since then, Guardian Angels have patrolled areas such as subways, shopping mall parking lots, concerts, public parks, and streets that are dangerous. As the streets are getting safer, the Guardian Angels are spending more time on safety education and programs for children in poor areas. They also have programs to help and **escort** senior citizens and people with disabilities so these people can participate in activities without fear. They have speakers who go out to schools and other organizations to talk about self-defense. Today, the Guardian Angels even include professional teachers and counselors for young people after school.

5 The Guardian Angels have become famous for making people feel safe in their neighborhoods. Nearly twenty years after this organization began, a woman asked Curtis Sliwa how he planned to make people feel safe **online**. Sliwa thought about that question, and he decided to start another program for a new problem: Internet crime. CyberAngels, Sliwa's program for online safety, started in 1995 and is the oldest and largest cyber-safety program. It's an information and help line for those who come across trouble through the Internet, or those who want to make sure they never do. It combats Internet crime like viruses, **fraud**, and online behavior that threatens people or hurts children. By working with **law enforcement** agencies, the group has been instrumental in catching criminals associated with the Internet. CyberAngels also provide classes on Internet issues for parents, teachers, librarians, and the general public so they can take advantage of the vast **resources** of the Internet in safety.

6 Anyone, male or female, can become a CyberAngel or Guardian Angel, but these organizations have other special requirements for their volunteers. CyberAngels must be at least eighteen years old, and they must pass a background check. The group especially needs the services of skilled workers such as law enforcement workers, teachers, computer experts, and people in the legal field. Not everyone who wants to be a CyberAngel is accepted. Guardian Angels also have high expectations of their volunteers. They must be at least sixteen years old, have no serious criminal record, and be going to school, working, or able to prove how they support themselves otherwise. After the organization looks at an applicant's background, he or she must complete a training program that lasts ten hours a week for three months. There is training in self-defense, first aid, the legal code, how to make a citizen's arrest, and how to patrol. It is not necessary to be a martial arts expert to become a Guardian Angel. **Attitude** and dedication are more important than anything else.

However, it helps if you know how to defend yourself. Once they are trained, members have to make two patrols a week, which totals about eight hours. The Guardian Angels do not carry weapons. Before they go out on patrol, each member is searched for weapons and drugs just to make sure. If they are found to have any of these, they are immediately **dismissed**.

7 As nonprofit organizations, Guardian Angels and CyberAngels do not receive money from the government or big corporations. Angels do not get a salary; they are all voluntary workers. The organization gets some money from individual contributions to help in communities that need them. Today, the organization has 5,000 members in 67 cities in the United States, Canada, and Mexico. Popular support of Guardian Angels has grown in other parts of the world, too, and over twenty chapters or groups have been created around the world. The first Guardian Angel chapter outside the United States was started in London, and now there are additional European chapters in Nottingham, England, and Milan, Italy. In South America, there are Guardian Angels in Rio de Janeiro, Brazil, and we can also find them in several cities in Japan.

8 The Guardian Angels and CyberAngels spread the idea of taking responsibility and becoming a power for good. Their actions have improved the lives of the people they serve—especially young people—as well as those of the volunteers themselves. For over twenty-five years, their idea has inspired young people. Now, it continues to do so as it spreads around the world.

VOCABULARY

MEANING

Circle the letter of the answer that is closest in meaning to the underlined word.

1. A man begged him to do something about the street <u>muggers</u>.
   a. robbers
   b. workers
   c. fighters
   d. beggars

2. Sliwa's program combats Internet crime like viruses, <u>fraud</u>, and online behavior that threatens people.

   a. foolish actions

   b. violent actions

   c. dishonest actions

   d. rude actions

3. The Rock Brigade started to improve the <u>deteriorated</u> neighborhood.

   a. not clean

   b. unpopular

   c. in bad condition

   d. crowded with buildings

4. If the volunteers are found to have weapons or drugs, they are immediately <u>dismissed</u>.

   a. reported

   b. sent away

   c. put in jail

   d. criticized

5. The CyberAngels provide classes on Internet issues so people can take advantage of the vast <u>resources</u> of the Internet.

   a. methods of doing things

   b. places to visit

   c. ways to get training

   d. sources of information or support

6. A retired <u>transit</u> worker begged him to do something.

   a. related to moving people from one place to another

   b. related to changing speech from one language to another

   c. related to passing from one object to another

   d. related to sending signals from one thing to another

7. <u>Attitude</u> and dedication are more important than anything else.

   a. a way of fighting or defending oneself

   b. a way of speaking

   c. a way of listening to others

   d. a way of feeling or thinking

8. They also have programs to help and <u>escort</u> senior citizens.
   a. talk with someone
   b. care for someone
   c. go with someone
   d. entertain someone

9. The city had no money to <u>hire</u> police.
   a. teach someone a skill
   b. pay someone for working
   c. organize people into groups
   d. improve living conditions for people

10. A woman asked Sliwa how he planned to make people feel safe <u>online</u>.
   a. connected to the Internet
   b. on the telephone
   c. on the street
   d. in their homes

WORDS THAT GO TOGETHER

A. Find words in the reading that go together with the words below to make phrases.

1. volunteer _____
2. at _____
3. _____ the subway
4. sneak _____
5. _____ enforcement
6. infested _____
7. _____ your e-mail

B. Complete the sentences with the phrases from Part A.

1. If you _____ someplace, you enter it secretly without anyone seeing you.
2. When a group of people get together and offer their services and help to others without payment, they are a _____.
3. If a building or area is _____ something, it means that there is too much of something bad which is causing trouble.

4. To _____ is to get on a railroad system that has trains running under the ground.

5. If you are _____, you are connecting to the Internet to see whether you have any electronic messages.

6. _____ means "in any way."

7. _____ groups, such as police, make people obey the law by using force or the threat of force.

C. Now use the phrases in your own sentences.

Example: *Many people in my office* ride the subway *to work every morning.*

USE

Work with a partner to answer the questions. Use complete sentences.

1. What is the name of a *volunteer organization* that exists in your community or country?

2. When was the last time you had to *escort* someone to a place or event?

3. Which city do you think has a lot of *muggers*?

4. What does a *deteriorated* neighborhood look like?

5. If you were going to *hire* a worker, what kind of qualities would you expect that person to have?

6. Have you ever been somewhere that wasn't safe *at all*? Explain the place or situation.

7. What kind of *attitude* helps a person to be successful?

COMPREHENSION

UNDERSTANDING MAIN IDEAS

Circle the letter of the best answer.

1. The main idea of paragraph 3 is that _____.

   a. although crime had increased in New York, the city had no money to hire the police needed to control crime

   b. the Guardian Angels would find muggers and then hold them until the police came to arrest them

c. the Guardian Angels began with thirteen volunteers, including Sliwa, and were known as the "Magnificent Thirteen"

d. the Guardian Angels expanded their program from cleaning up the neighborhood to making it safer

2. The main idea of paragraph 4 is that _____.

   a. the Guardian Angels patrol such areas as subways, shopping mall parking lots, concerts, public parks, and dangerous streets

   b. the Guardian Angels include professional teachers and counselors for young people after school

   c. now the Guardian Angels spend less time on the street and more time on education, safety, and community programs

   d. the Guardian Angels have speakers who go out to schools and other organizations to talk about self-defense

3. The main idea of paragraph 5 is that _____.

   a. in 1995, Sliwa started the CyberAngels to combat Internet crime

   b. nearly twenty years after the founding of the Guardian Angels, a woman asked Sliwa how he planned to make people feel safe online

   c. CyberAngels is an information and help line for those who come across trouble on the Internet

   d. the CyberAngels provide classes on Internet issues for parents, teachers, librarians, and the general public

4. The main idea of paragraph 6 is that _____.

   a. if you are a volunteer for the CyberAngels or the Guardian Angels, you should know how to defend yourself

   b. volunteers for the CyberAngels or the Guardian Angels must meet special requirements and receive training

   c. not everyone who wants to be a CyberAngel is accepted

   d. all Guardian Angel volunteers are searched for weapons and drugs before they go out on patrol

REMEMBERING DETAILS

Reread the passage and fill in the blanks.

1. The first Guardian Angel chapter outside the United States was started in

    _____.

2. The Rock Brigade improved the neighborhood by

    _____, _____, and

    _____.

3. One Guardian Angel community program helps to escort

    _____ and _____.

4. The CyberAngels need the services of skilled workers such as

    _____, _____,

    _____, and _____.

5. Your computer can receive a virus through an _____.

6. A transit worker begged Sliwa to do something about the

    _____.

7. To be a Guardian Angel, you do not have to be an expert in the

    _____.

8. The Guardian Angels have become famous for _____ in
    their neighborhoods.

MAKING INFERENCES

**Some of the following statements can be inferred, or guessed, from the reading and
others cannot. Circle the number of each statement that can be inferred.**

1. You don't know when your computer is receiving a virus.
2. Curtis Sliwa started the Rock Brigade because he wanted to be a police
    officer.
3. Curtis Sliwa and his twelve volunteers helped the police make the streets
    safer.
4. There are criminals online just as there are criminals in the streets.
5. The Guardian Angels have always helped the poor and senior citizens.
6. It is easy for anyone to become a member of the Guardian Angels.
7. The Guardian Angels plan to start chapters in every country in the world.
8. The Guardian Angels organization does not have the popularity that it
    had twenty-five years ago.

DISCUSSION

Discuss the answers to these questions with your classmates.

1. Are there any volunteer organizations that help people in your community? Who are they? What do they do?
2. Why are volunteer organizations important to society? Will there still be a need for them in the future? Why or why not?
3. Would your city be a good place for the Guardian Angels to go? Why or why not?
4. Would you like to be a Guardian Angel or CyberAngel? Why or why not?

WRITING

On separate paper, write a paragraph or an essay about one of the following topics:

1. Write about two advantages or disadvantages of the Internet.
2. What can the community or community services (police, social services) do to improve your neighborhood? State two or three possible improvements.
3. Do you agree or disagree with using volunteers or a volunteer organization to help stop or prevent crime in dangerous areas? Give reasons.

GRAMMAR AND PUNCTUATION

 ARTICLES: *A, AN, THE*

> ***Articles*** give information about a noun. We use *a / an* when the noun is not known to the reader or listener. We use *the* after we know what noun we are talking about. Therefore, we use *a / an* for the first reference and *the* for the next and other references. (Note: We use *an* before a vowel sound.)
>
> *CyberAngels is **an** organization.* (We use *a / an* because this is the first time we mention *organization*.)
>
> ***The** organization protects us from crime on the Internet.* (We use *the* because *organization* has been mentioned before.)
>
> **We use *the* or no article for plural nouns. We don't use an article when we refer to a group in general.**
>
> *Did you see **the muggers** the police arrested?* (specific)
>
> ***Muggers** are a problem in some neighborhoods.* (group in general)

Fill in the blanks with *the*, *a* or *an*, or *X* for no article.

1. Guardian Angels is _____ volunteer organization. _____ organization protects people from _____ neighborhood crimes.

2. You can go on _____ Internet from _____ computer.

3. There are _____ viruses and other types of crime on _____ Internet.

4. There may be _____ virus in one of _____ messages you receive in your e-mail.

5. CyberAngels is _____ organization that protects _____ citizens from Internet crime.

6. CyberAngels also gives _____ classes to _____ general public on how to use _____ Internet.

7. CyberAngels works with _____ law enforcement agencies to catch _____ criminals.

8. To be _____ CyberAngel, you must pass _____ background check.

9. _____ males or _____ females are accepted to become _____ CyberAngels.

10. _____ person who commits Internet crime may go to _____ prison.

UNIT 10

Why Do People Want to Climb Mount Everest?

BEFORE YOU READ

Answer these questions.

1. Where is Mount Everest?
2. Who were the first men to successfully climb Mount Everest?
3. Why do people do dangerous things, such as climbing mountains?

Why Do People Want to Climb Mount Everest?

1 When asked why he wanted to climb Mount Everest, the famous words of the British climber George Mallory were, "Because it is there." Unfortunately, to this day we do not know if George Mallory and his partner Andrew Irvine made it to the top when they tried to climb Everest in 1924. They died in the **attempt**, and it was only recently—in 1999—that Mallory's body was found on the mountain. People were sad about Mallory and Irvine's disappearance, and that is when the **fascination with** Everest began. There are many reasons why people climb mountains, such as personal satisfaction, **prestige**, power, the difficulty, and the **risk**, but they may also do it to understand their **inner strength**. The first man known to have climbed a mountain for no reason other than it was there was Frenchman Antoine de Ville. In 1492, he climbed a mountain in France (Mont Aiguille) and liked the view so much that he stayed there for six days.

2 Mount Everest, the highest mountain in the world, was named after Sir George Everest, a British surveyor in India who recorded the mountain's location in 1841. Mount Everest is in the Himalaya Mountains in Nepal. Its official height, which was determined using a Global Positioning System satellite in 1999, is 29,035 feet (8,850 meters). Until then, every time surveyors measured the mountain there was a difference of several feet. It was later found that the changing depth of ice at the **summit**, and not a mistake of the surveyors, was altering the mountain's height.

3 Many people had tried to climb Everest, but none were successful until 1953, when Edmund Hillary (later Sir Edmund Hillary) and Tenzing Norgay reached its summit. Edmund Hillary was from New Zealand, and Tenzing Norgay was a native Sherpa from Nepal. The Sherpas are skilled mountain climbers, and many of them are today's guides and porters in the expeditions to Everest.

4 Since 1953, many Everest records have been set by climbers who have tried the **unprecedented**. Ed Viesturs reached the summit without using extra oxygen. Junko Tabei was the first woman to reach the summit, and Lydia Bradley was the first woman to reach it without using extra oxygen. People with disabilities also have reached the mountaintop,

such as a blind man, a man with one arm, and a man with one leg. In 2003, a seventy-year-old man became the oldest person to reach the summit. People have skied and snowboarded from the summit, three brothers reached it on the same day, and one person climbed Everest to sleep there. He slept for 21 hours! Speed records also have been set. The most recent one was 10 hours 56 minutes.

5 Needless to say, with all these attempts there have been many accidents and deaths on Everest. A blizzard in May 1996 killed eight climbers in one day. These climbers were in the best **physical condition** and had laptop computers, satellite phones, and other advanced equipment to help them climb the mountain. We know that sixty people died in the 1990s alone. In fact, one of every thirty climbers attempting to reach the summit has died, and yet climbers continue to risk their lives.

6 Today Everest has lost some of its old **mystique** and **appeal** because so many people are reaching its top. Thousands of mountaineers pass through base camp every year, but don't go as far as the summit. Close to 2,000 climbers have reached the summit, coming from every possible route. On May 16, 2002, fifty-four climbers reached the top successfully on the same day! These days, climbing Mount Everest has become a **novelty** for those who are in good physical condition and can afford to pay as much as $65,000 for climbing guides and fees. There are only a few months in the year that weather conditions make it practical to climb the mountain. These are April, May, October, December, and January. As a result, people usually have to make plans **in advance** to climb Everest. At one point, there was a twelve-year wait! It looks like the highest mountain in the world is becoming quite crowded. On the mountain, there is usually a line of people **waiting their turn** to get to the top. Even Sir Edmund Hillary is not **pleased with** the crowds. He said that if he were younger, he would not want to be in an expedition with so many people around.

7 Communication has always been a problem in such a remote area as Nepal. The nearest telephones from base camp, which is at 17,000 feet (5,182 meters), are a four-day walk away. These days, most trekkers (people who go on long and difficult walks) use satellite phones to run Web sites to contact their friends and family at home. Recently, someone had a better idea. A Sherpa, the grandson of a man from Nepal who was in the first expedition fifty years ago, plans to make an Internet café at

the base camp of Everest. This will be the highest Internet café in the world! He is waiting for permission from the government to **go ahead with** the project. The money from the café will go to a project to clean up the tons of garbage left behind by the tens of thousands of tourists that come to Nepal every year.

8 Each of these tourists has his or her own reasons for climbing Everest. For many, the more **challenging** the mountain, the more they like it. These people know they risk their lives, but they don't mind. However, for many extreme climbers today, reaching the top of Mount Everest is not the challenge it once was, because too many people have done it. Many climbers want to go where no one has **dared**. Though it may be true that Mount Everest has lost some of its mystique, it is still the highest mountain on Earth. For this reason, it will probably always attract many of the world's best climbers.

VOCABULARY

MEANING

Circle the letter of the answer that is closest in meaning to the underlined word.

1. It was later found that the changing depth of ice at the <u>summit</u> was altering the mountain's height.
   a. bottom
   b. top
   c. middle
   d. end

2. Today, Everest has lost some of its old <u>mystique</u>.
   a. quality that makes something special
   b. quality that makes something dangerous
   c. quality that makes something popular
   d. quality that makes something beautiful

3. For many, the more <u>challenging</u> the mountain, the more they like it.
   a. difficult
   b. distant
   c. mysterious
   d. large

4. There are many reasons why people climb mountains, such as <u>prestige</u>, power, and the difficulty.
   a. happiness
   b. satisfaction
   c. fame
   d. health

5. Since 1953, many Everest records have been set by climbers who have tried the <u>unprecedented</u>.
   a. actions that are very dangerous
   b. actions that require strength to do
   c. actions that have never been done before
   d. actions that other people have done in the past

6. Today, Everest has lost some of its old <u>appeal</u>.
   a. beauty
   b. difficulty
   c. danger
   d. interest

7. Many climbers want to go where no one has <u>dared</u>.
   a. been scared to go
   b. been brave enough to go
   c. wanted to go
   d. had the desire to go

8. There are many reasons why people climb mountains, such as the power, difficulty, and <u>risk</u>.
   a. enjoyment
   b. danger
   c. reward
   d. excitement

9. These days, climbing Mount Everest has become a <u>novelty</u>.
   a. something beautiful and charming
   b. something difficult and dangerous
   c. something big and costly
   d. something new and unusual

10. Mallory and Irvine died in the <u>attempt</u>.
    a. experience
    b. emotion
    c. effort
    d. climb

 WORDS THAT GO TOGETHER

A. Find words in the reading that go together with the words below to make phrases.

1. _____ their turn
2. _____ ahead _____
3. fascination _____
4. physical _____
5. _____ strength
6. pleased _____
7. _____ advance

B. Complete the sentences with the phrases from Part A.

1. To have a _____ something is to have a powerful interest in it.

2. To be _____ something is to be satisfied and happy with it.

3. When pcople are _____, they can't do something because there are people in front of them who have to do it first.

4. The health and strength of your body, whether good or bad, is your _____.

5. To act _____ is to prepare for something before it happens.

6. When you _____ something, you begin or continue it.

7. Your bravery, courage, and mental ability to overcome pain and fear are all part of your _____.

C. Now use the phrases in your own sentences.

Example: *People who eat healthy foods and exercise every day are usually in good*
         physical condition.

USE

Work with a partner to answer the questions. Use complete sentences.

1. What are two things that you usually need to do *in advance* when you go on a trip?
2. What are two types of accomplishments that bring people *prestige*?
3. Where can you often see people *waiting their turn*?
4. What is a place that has *mystique* for many people?
5. Where would you likely see people in excellent *physical condition*?
6. What are two sports that involve some *risk*?
7. What activity is physically *challenging*?
8. What famous place has an *appeal* to you?

COMPREHENSION

UNDERSTANDING MAIN IDEAS

Circle the letter of the best answer.

1. Paragraph 4 is mainly about how _____.
   a. a seventy-year-old man became the oldest person to reach the summit of Everest
   b. people have skied and snowboarded from the summit
   c. climbers have set many different records on Mount Everest
   d. people with disabilities have reached the summit

2. The main idea of paragraph 5 is _____.
   a. over the years, there have been many accidents and deaths on Everest
   b. in 1996, eight climbers were killed in one day, even though they had computers and phones with them
   c. sixty people died on Everest in the 1990s alone
   d. one in every thirty climbers attempting to reach the summit of Mount Everest has died

3. The main idea of paragraph 6 is that _____.

   a. climbing Mount Everest has become a novelty for those who are in good physical condition and can afford to pay for guides and fees

   b. there are only a few months in the year that weather conditions make it practical to climb Mount Everest

   c. climbing Mount Everest has become so popular that the crowded mountain is losing some of its appeal

   d. Sir Edmund Hillary is not pleased with the crowds on Mount Everest

4. The main idea of paragraph 7 is _____.

   a. the nearest phones from the base camp are a four-day walk away

   b. many trekkers use satellite phones to contact their friends and family

   c. the money from an Internet café would go to a project to clean up tons of garbage left behind by climbers on Mount Everest

   d. a Sherpa plans to solve the communication problem on Everest by opening an Internet café

REMEMBERING DETAILS

Reread the passage and fill in the blanks.

1. The months in which weather conditions allow people to climb Everest are _____, _____, _____, _____, and _____.

2. The first man known to climb a mountain for no reason was _____, in the year _____.

3. The first woman to reach the summit of Mount Everest was _____.

4. The official height of Everest is _____; it was determined using a _____ in 1999.

5. Mount Everest is located in _____ in the country of _____.

6. The number of climbers who have reached the summit of Everest is _____.

7. The base camp of Mount Everest is located at a height of _____.

8. Edmund Hillary was a climber from _____, while Tenzing Norgay was a _____ from _____.

MAKING INFERENCES

The answers to these questions can be inferred, or guessed, from the reading. Circle the letter of the best answer.

1. The reading implies that Mallory and Irvine _____.
   a. couldn't have made it to the top of Everest
   b. didn't try to make it to the summit of Everest
   c. may possibly have made it to the top of Everest
   d. tried to climb Everest for scientific reasons

2. It can be inferred from the reading that _____.
   a. most climbers can make it to the summit of Everest without the help of guides
   b. most climbers need extra oxygen to make it to the summit of Everest
   c. most climbers can climb to the summit without extra oxygen
   d. only young people in top physical condition can make it to the summit

3. From the reading, it can be concluded that _____.
   a. even with the help of modern technology, climbing Everest is still dangerous
   b. because of modern technology, climbing Everest is no longer dangerous
   c. fewer people are killed or hurt on Everest now than in the 1950s
   d. the weather isn't a cause in the accidents and deaths on Everest

4. The reading implies that _____.
   a. most people who climb Everest have been climbing mountains all their lives
   b. even inexperienced climbers can reach the summit of Everest
   c. most people are not willing to wait years to climb Everest
   d. though many people try to climb Everest, few make it to the summit

5. It can be inferred from the reading that _____.
   a. climbers on Everest have no way to contact people at home
   b. an Internet café on Everest will probably never be used
   c. climbers on Everest aren't interested in what Sir Edmund Hillary did in 1953
   d. the number of climbers on Everest is causing some problems with the environment

DISCUSSION

Discuss the answers to these questions with your classmates.

1. Would you like to climb Mount Everest? Why or why not?
2. What are some places in your country where people go to challenge themselves?
3. Why are more people doing dangerous activities now than ever before?
4. Do you think that building an Internet café on Everest is a good idea? Why or why not?

WRITING

On separate paper, write a paragraph or an essay about one of the following topics:

1. What is the greatest challenge in your life. Why is it a challenge? What would you do once you faced or overcame the challenge?
2. What accomplishments have you had or would you like to have? Explain.
3. What is your favorite sport? Give two or three reasons.

GRAMMAR AND PUNCTUATION

 THE DEFINITE ARTICLE: GEOGRAPHICAL NAMES AND DIRECTIONS

1. **We use the definite article (*the*) with:**

   • groups of geographical features, such as mountain ranges, lakes, and islands, but not with the names of most single features. We <u>do</u> use *the* with names of single rivers and oceans.

   > *the* Himalayas, *the* Great Lakes   <u>but</u>   Mount Everest, Lake Superior
   > *the* Ganges River, *the* Pacific Ocean

   • plural names of countries, but not singular names of countries.

   > *the* United States, *the* Philippines   <u>but</u>   Japan, Canada

2. **For directions on the compass, we say:**

   > *the* north of India   <u>but</u>   northern India

We also say *the* Middle East and *the* Far East, but we use directions without *the* in names of some countries and regions:

North America   South Africa

(Note: In most maps, *the* is <u>not</u> included in names.)

Rewrite the incorrect sentences. Write *the* where necessary.

1. Africa's highest mountain is the Mount Kilimanjaro.

   _____

2. Kilimanjaro is in the eastern Africa.

   _____

3. Himalayas are in north of India.

   _____

4. The Andros Island is the largest in the Bahamas.

   _____

5. Nile River flows from Lake Victoria in the Uganda into Mediterranean Sea in Egypt.

   _____

6. The Mount Blanc is the highest mountain in Alps.

   _____

7. The Rockies is the name of the mountain range in the west of the North America.

   _____

8. Hebrides Islands are in Atlantic Ocean along the western Scotland.

   _____

9. The Andes Mountains and Amazon River are both found in the South America.

   _____

10. Philippines is in Far East.

   _____

UNIT 11

Why Is the Renaissance Important?

BEFORE YOU READ

Answer these questions.

1. Who are some great artists in your country's past or present?
2. Who are some famous writers?
3. Who are some famous scientists?

Why Is the Renaissance Important?

1 During the period of the Middle Ages (from about 500 C.E. to the mid–1400s) there were no great changes in the **way of life** in Europe. People did what their fathers did before them, and there were few new inventions or discoveries. Most people believed in what they were told and did not care about anything outside their lives. One reason for this may be because only a few people received an education, and books were scarce. Then, a change began. People became better educated, trade and industry developed, the arts **flourished**, and explorers discovered new lands. We call this great change the Renaissance, which in French means "rebirth." The Renaissance, which took place in Europe between the thirteenth and sixteenth centuries, was a new **stage** in the history of the world.

2 Some people think that the Renaissance got started when the Turks took over the Greek city Constantinople (now Istanbul) in 1453. Greek scholars left Constantinople and settled in other parts of Europe. In these new locations, they taught Greek and shared their precious books. The study of classical Greek and Roman writers and thinkers began again, and a new desire for learning spread throughout Europe.

3 People began to inquire into everything, and some began to question their beliefs and ways of thinking. In Germany, Martin Luther started a revolt against the **conventions** of the Roman Catholic Church. Soon, other Christians agreed that the Church needed to change, and several new Christian religions were established.

4 Other people began to think about new types of government that were based on the democratic values of ancient Greece. Italy, the birthplace of the Renaissance, was organized into city-states that governed themselves. Though wealthy families and the Church held much of the power in these areas, the city-states were moving a step **in the direction of** government by the people. The most famous political thinker of the Renaissance was Niccolo Machiavelli. In his book on government entitled *The Prince*, he stated that a good leader could do bad and dishonest things in order to **preserve** his power and protect his government. Though people in his own time thought that Machiavelli was evil for saying these things, his book is now famous and modern political thinkers respect some of his ideas.

5 The "new learning" taught people to think in new ways, and it also **encouraged** gifted people to paint pictures, make statues and buildings, and write great literature. In fact, some of the best artists of the day did all of these things. As a result, when a person today is skilled in many areas, he or she is often called a "Renaissance man" or a "Renaissance woman."

6 The artistic developments of the Renaissance first happened in the Italian city of Florence, and then they spread to other Italian cities. **As a result of** trade and banking, cities like Florence, Venice, and Milan became very wealthy, and their rich citizens had both the time and money to enjoy music, art, and poetry. These cities produced great painters and sculptors, like Michelangelo, Leonardo da Vinci, and Raphael. These artists created some of history's finest **works of art**. For example, Michelangelo spent four years painting thousands of feet of curved ceiling in the Vatican's Sistine Chapel. To do this, he had to learn a whole new style of painting. He also had to paint lying on his back beneath the ceiling as paint dripped down onto his face. Despite these **obstacles**, he created one of art's greatest masterpieces.

7 A new kind of architecture also began in the Renaissance. It **blended** the old, classical styles with new ideas. Again, it started in Florence. A cathedral there had been started in 1296, but it remained unfinished for over 100 years because no one could figure out how to build the curved roof that it needed. Then architect Filippo Brunelleschi invented a new type of dome that was higher and grander than any from the classical **era**. The dome **marks** the beginning of Renaissance architecture.

8 From Italy, interest in the arts and new ways of thinking spread to other countries. The Netherlands became famous for great painters; England produced many writers, including William Shakespeare; and Spain had the literature of Cervantes. The new **passion for** learning also led to amazing discoveries in science by Galileo, Kepler, and Newton. Some of these findings went against the most basic beliefs of the time. For example, Galileo's discovery that the sun, not the Earth, was the center of the solar system got him into serious trouble with many religious people. They forced him to say that he had been wrong about his discovery, even though he knew he was right.

9 The development of the printing press in Germany by a man named Johannes Gutenberg helped more than anything to spread the new ideas

of the Renaissance. Before that time, books were scarce and very expensive because they were written by hand. Gutenberg discovered how to use a moveable metal type, and his first book was published in 1455. Printing was a very important invention. With it, books were made more cheaply and quickly than ever. In addition, most books had been written in Latin before, as this was thought to be the language of study. However, with the Renaissance, the middle classes could now afford books, and they wanted books in their own languages. They also wanted a greater variety of things to read, such as books on travel, poetry, and romance. Printing helped make the works of the best writers and all kinds of knowledge available to all.

10 About the time printing was discovered, sailors were **setting out** on voyages of discovery. Now that the Turks were masters of the eastern Mediterranean, it was no longer possible to trade with India by the old land route. A new way had to be found, perhaps by sailing around the coast of Africa—or perhaps by sailing around the world! There were many explorers around this time, including Columbus, Vasco de Gama, Cabot, Magellan, and Drake. Representing countries throughout Europe, these men sailed new waters and discovered new lands, including the Americas. With all this travel, tools for exploration and navigation improved, and better ships were made. As people traveled, they gained new ideas that helped to change their way of living. For example, Europeans now wanted goods—such as spices, silk, and gold—from far away countries.

11 The Renaissance didn't begin suddenly when Constantinople was taken over by the Turks or when the first book was printed in 1455. Forces that **brought** it **about** had been developing for many years as Europeans began to desire and gain new knowledge. From this new learning came the great changes that we call the Renaissance. These advancements—from the discovery of printing to a renewed interest in art and literature and the discovery of new lands—**affected** almost every area of European life. They also formed the basis for many parts of our modern life and beliefs. This is why some people think of the Renaissance as the beginning of modern history.

VOCABULARY

MEANING

Circle the letter of the answer that is closest in meaning to the underlined word.

1. Martin Luther started a revolt against the <u>conventions</u> of the Roman Catholic Church.
   a. writings
   b. leaders
   c. speeches
   d. customs

2. Despite these <u>obstacles</u>, he created one of art's greatest masterpieces.
   a. methods
   b. changes
   c. difficulties
   d. differences

3. It <u>blended</u> the old, classical styles with new ideas.
   a. mixed together
   b. took apart
   c. put side by side
   d. put one over the other

4. The Renaissance was a new <u>stage</u> in the history of the world.
   a. special event
   b. long period of time
   c. step in development
   d. type of belief

5. The dome <u>marks</u> the beginning of Renaissance architecture.
   a. makes a statement about
   b. serves as a sign of
   c. gives an example of
   d. tells a story about

6. During the Renaissance, the arts <u>flourished</u>.
    a. grew and improved
    b. were almost forgotten
    c. were not accepted
    d. stayed about the same

7. In his book on government entitled *The Prince,* Machiavelli stated that a good leader could do bad and dishonest things in order to <u>preserve</u> his power.
    a. put out of sight of others
    b. keep safe and unchanged
    c. make larger and stronger
    d. take away from

8. Brunelleschi invented a new type of dome that was higher and grander than any from the classical <u>era</u>.
    a. a particular area of the world
    b. a set of years in history
    c. a certain style of art
    d. a certain group of people

9. These advancements <u>affected</u> almost every area of European life.
    a. created
    b. defeated
    c. built up
    d. changed

10. The "new learning" <u>encouraged</u> gifted people to paint pictures.
    a. honored by important people
    b. ordered to change
    c. helped to become confident
    d. warned about other people

WORDS THAT GO TOGETHER

A. Find words in the reading that go together with the words below to make phrases.

1. _____ of art
2. way of _____
3. setting _____
4. _____ a result _____
5. brought . . . _____
6. passion _____
7. _____ the direction _____

B. Complete the sentences with the phrases from Part A.

1. When you have strong and deep feelings for something, you have a
   _____ it.
2. When something happens because of an action or event, it happens
   _____ it.
3. _____ are objects that are produced by painting,
   writing, sculpting, and other creative skills.
4. If you are on a course toward something, you are moving _____ it.
5. The normal experiences and activities of a group or culture are its
   _____.
6. If something caused an event to happen, then that thing
   _____ the event _____.
7. If you are beginning a trip, you are _____ on a journey.

C. Now use the phrases in your own sentences.

Example: As a result of *the bad weather, we had to cancel our hiking trip.*

USE

Work with a partner to answer the questions. Use complete sentences.

1. What are two of your favorite *works of art*?
2. When was the last time you *encouraged* someone to do something?
3. How is the *way of life* in your country different from that in another place
   you've been to?
4. What is a historical event that greatly *affected* the people in your country?
5. If you were *setting out* on a journey, where would you like to be going?

6. What part of nature would you like to *preserve* for future generations?
7. What is your favorite *era* in history?
8. Who is a historical figure that overcame many *obstacles* in his or her life?

COMPREHENSION

UNDERSTANDING MAIN IDEAS

Some of the following statements are main ideas, and some are supporting statements. Some of them are stated directly in the reading. Find the statements. Write *M* for each main idea. Write *S* for each supporting statement.

_____ 1. During the period of the Middle Ages (from about 500 C.E. to the mid–1400s) there were no great changes in the way of life in Europe.

_____ 2. Most people believed in what they were told and did not care for anything outside their lives.

_____ 3. The Renaissance, which took place in Europe between the thirteenth and sixteenth centuries, was a new stage in the history of the world.

_____ 4. The most famous political thinker of the Renaissance was Niccolo Machiavelli.

_____ 5. The artistic developments of the Renaissance first happened in the Italian city of Florence, and then they spread to other Italian cities.

_____ 6. Forces that brought about the Renaissance had been developing for many years as Europeans began to desire and gain new knowledge.

_____ 7. Advancements in the Renaissance also formed the basis for many parts of our modern life and beliefs.

REMEMBERING DETAILS

Reread the passage and answer the questions. Write complete sentences.

1. What did Michelangelo spend four years painting?

_____

2. Who are three Renaissance scientists who made great discoveries?

_____

3. Who developed the printing press, and what country was he from?

_____

4. Who were five famous explorers of the Renaissance?

   _____

5. What does the word *Renaissance* mean, and what language is it from?

   _____

6. What does it mean when a person today is called a "Renaissance man" or a "Renaissance woman"?

   _____

7. What is the name of the architect who invented a new type of dome, and where was the cathedral for which he designed this dome?

   _____

8. In what language had most books been written before the Renaissance?

   _____

MAKING INFERENCES

The answers to these questions can be inferred, or guessed, from the reading. Circle the letter of the best answer.

1. The reading implies that before the Renaissance _____.
   a. people were eager to learn new things
   b. education was limited to scholars and privileged people
   c. people wanted to change their lives but couldn't
   d. middle-class people did a lot of reading

2. It can be inferred from the reading that _____.
   a. Turkish scholars spread their knowledge throughout Europe
   b. German philosophers were responsible for starting the Renaissance
   c. The Greeks had a strong influence on Renaissance thinking
   d. France was the birthplace of the Renaissance

3. From the reading, it can be concluded that the Renaissance _____.
   a. made people afraid to go against traditional beliefs
   b. influenced people to fight against each other
   c. helped leaders to maintain control over the middle class
   d. caused people to make changes in their lives

4. The reading implies that during the Renaissance _____.
   a. economic prosperity was important to the development of the arts
   b. people were poor, but they still appreciated their artists
   c. there were many artists, but their works were not enjoyed by most people
   d. Italy was the only country that encouraged artists to produce new styles of art

5. It can be inferred from the reading that the major causes of the Renaissance were _____.
   a. explorations of new lands
   b. new artists and writers who created great works
   c. reading and learning
   d. changes in government

DISCUSSION

Discuss the answers to these questions with your classmates.

1. What do you think are the three most important inventions in the history of the world?
2. What do you think was the greatest period in the history of your country? Why?
3. Do you think that art and literature are important in modern society? Why or why not?
4. Do you agree with Machiavelli's idea that a good leader can do bad and dishonest things in order to preserve his power and protect his government? Why or why not?

WRITING

On separate paper, write a paragraph or an essay about one of the following topics:

1. What is an invention that you think is important in your life? Give three reasons why it is important.
2. How have methods of study and learning changed in the last ten years? Are these methods better than those in the past or not?
3. What is one advancement in the field of medicine or science that has changed people's lives? State three ways it has helped people.

GRAMMAR AND PUNCTUATION

SHOWING CONTRAST: *THOUGH, ALTHOUGH; DESPITE, IN SPITE OF*

1. **To show contrast or an unexpected result, we can use *although* or *though* to begin a subordinate (adverb) clause. The subordinate clause can come before or after the main clause; the meaning is the same. (*Though* is less formal than *although*.)**

   Although people once thought Machiavelli was evil for saying these things, his book is now respected by political thinkers.

   *Machiavelli's book is now respected by political thinkers, **though** people once thought he was evil for saying these things.*

2. **We can also use the prepositions *despite* and *in spite of* to express contrast. They usually are followed by a noun.**

   Despite these obstacles, Michelangelo created one of art's greatest masterpieces.

   In spite of these obstacles, Michelangelo created one of art's greatest masterpieces.

A. **Using the contrast word or phrase in parentheses, write a new sentence similar to the phrases and sentences below.**

1. China was more advanced, the Renaissance began in Europe. (*although*)

   _____

2. Galileo's belief that the Sun was the center of the universe. He said he was wrong. (*despite*)

   _____

3. Most people think El Greco was Spanish. He was Greek. (*though*)

   _____

4. Our association of the Renaissance with art. Explorers and scientists were also a part of the Renaissance. (*in spite of*)

   _____

B. **Now write three sentences of your own using a contrast word or phrase.**

1. _____

2. _____

3. _____

UNIT 12

What Is the Most Popular Sport in the World?

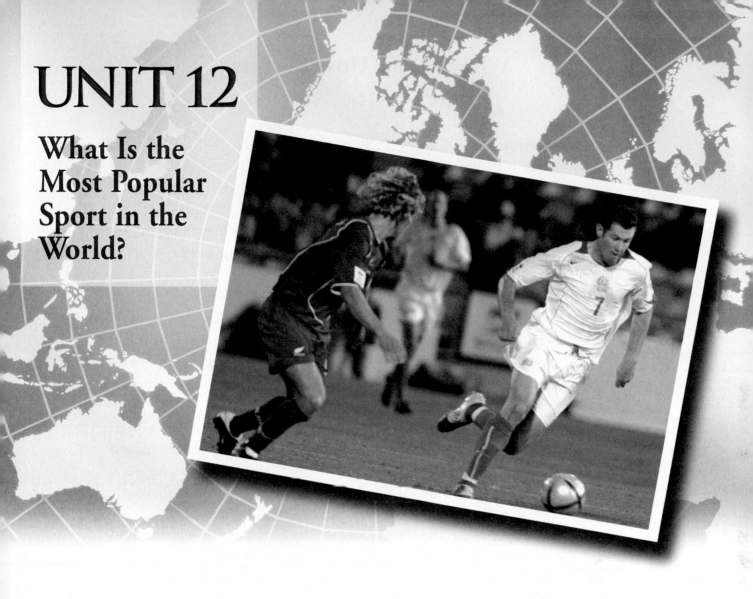

BEFORE YOU READ

Answer these questions.

1. What is the most popular sport in your country?
2. What sports do you like? Which do you play?
3. Who are some famous sports star of the past and present?

What Is the Most Popular Sport in the World?

1 Soccer—which is called football in most places—is the world's most popular sport. It is played in parks, fields, schools, and streets all over the world. It has about 250 million male and female players in more than 200 countries, and it has even more fans. In fact, an estimated 33 billion people around the world watched the 2004 World Cup tournament, making it the world's most watched television **sporting event**—it even **surpasses** the Olympics.

2 The exact origins of modern soccer are unknown. However, records show that the Chinese and Japanese played similar games over 2,000 years ago. Later, the ancient Greeks and Romans played it. The Romans took the game to Britain, which became the undisputed birthplace of modern soccer.

3 In Britain, the game came to be called football, because only the players' feet could touch the ball. However, when the British played football, it was more like war than a game. Towns and villages played against each other, and sometimes up to 500 people played on each team. There were even annual contests where large groups ran wildly from village to village playing the game. One game could last all day. Naturally, many people died and were injured. Several kings **banned** the game, passing laws against the sport because it was so rough and because soldiers preferred to play it than to **concentrate on** military training. Even Queen Elizabeth I had players in London put into jail because they caused so much damage to shops and **public property** when they played in the streets. But the game was too popular to be stopped.

4 Football was played in many English schools as early as the 1800s, but it had no formal rules. Later, two sets of rules were developed. One set was **devised** at a school called Rugby, where players could handle and run with the ball. The game of rugby developed from these rules. Other schools preferred the "hands-free" game. In 1848, the general rules of the hands-free game were established at Cambridge University.

5 The Football Association of England was formed in 1863. At that time, university students created slang by adding *–er* to words they shortened. The name soccer developed from adding *–er* to the letters *S*, *O*, and *C* (from the word *Association*). However, the game is still known

as football in most parts of the world **besides** North America, where *soccer* is more commonly used. Football quickly became popular throughout Europe and South America, and in 1900 it became one of the first **team sports** played in the Olympic Games. In 1904, seven nations— Belgium, Spain, Sweden, France, the Netherlands, Denmark, and Switzerland—met in Paris to form FIFA, the Federation Internationale de Football Association. FIFA has been the governing body of the sport **ever since**. Today, it has 204 member countries. Every four years, the world's strongest national football teams compete to be world champions and to get the World Cup—a golden trophy. The World Cup started in 1930. Beginning in 1958, it was held **alternately** in Europe and the Americas, but since 1996 it has been held in Asian countries as well.

6 Traditionally, football had been a game for male players, but now it has become popular with female players. Though women played football in China about 2,000 years ago, this was not heard of again until the game reappeared in the country's **school curriculum** for girls in the 1920s. **Appropriately**, the first Women's World Cup was held in China in 1991.

7 Throughout history, football was considered "unsuitable for women" in Europe, and they were banned from playing it. However, in the 1970s women were allowed to play again, and the sport's popularity started to grow. Certainly, this **trend** will continue. Since 1996, women's football has been included in the Olympic Games, and today more than 7 million young girls play in the United States alone. The United States is a newcomer to the women's game, but has won the World Cup twice and has also won two Olympic gold medals and one silver medal. Other new nations for women's football include Brazil, Nigeria, and Japan. The players of the American team were the first women players to be paid as full-time professionals, but now other countries are following their lead. Though salaries are over $100,000 a year for the top female professionals, they are nowhere near the average of $5 million that their male **counterparts** make.

8 Every country thinks it has the best football team, but they all admit that Brazil is the world's greatest football-playing country. The sport was first introduced to Brazil by a British man named Charles Miller, who started a team there. In 1899, this team played the country's first recorded game of football. Today, football is a way of life in Brazil. The Brazilian team was the first team to win the World Cup five times, and it has more professional teams than any other country in the world. Its talented

players, such as Pelé, Garrincha, Zico, and many others, have made Brazil famous throughout the world. These players **started out** very poor and became incredibly wealthy. They became true idols. Their influence can be seen on the young boys in the streets of poor neighborhoods throughout Brazil. The dream of nearly every young boy growing up in poverty there is to become a professional football player one day. It seems to be their only way of escape from poverty, and thus this sport has a greater influence on their lives than almost anything else.

9 Brazil is not the only country with football stars. Britain's David Beckham has become an idol for many young people. They read magazines about him and wait for his latest hairstyle to copy. In Tokyo, a giant three-meter (nearly ten-foot) statue of Beckham made **entirely** of chocolate was made to **promote** a new kind of chocolate. Advertisers use him to sell many things, and of course he makes millions of dollars from each advertising contract.

10 Football is the one of the oldest sports in the world. It has been gaining fans across the globe for over 2,000 years, and it doesn't show any signs of stopping. Will football continue to be the most popular sport in the world? Most people think it will!

VOCABULARY

 MEANING

Circle the letter of the answer that is closest in meaning to the underlined word.

1. One set of rules was <u>devised</u> at a school called Rugby.
    a. made up
    b. thrown out
    c. agreed to
    d. added to

2. Beginning in 1958, the World Cup was held <u>alternately</u> in Europe and the Americas.
    a. at the same time
    b. once only
    c. happening one after the other
    d. every two years

3. It even <u>surpasses</u> the Olympics.
   a. goes beyond
   b. stays about the same as
   c. is less than
   d. becomes a part of

4. Female players' salaries are nowhere near the average of $5 million that their male <u>counterparts</u> make.
   a. those in a different position
   b. those in the same position
   c. those in a lower position
   d. those in a higher position

5. A giant statue of Beckham was made to <u>promote</u> a new kind of chocolate.
   a. stop the use of
   b. create a new use for
   c. prepare the way for
   d. help the success of

6. Certainly, this <u>trend</u> will continue.
   a. change of plan or action
   b. general course or direction
   c. new arrangement or idea
   d. special place or situation

7. Several kings <u>banned</u> the game.
   a. tried to support
   b. liked to play
   c. said to stop
   d. believed in

8. A giant statue of Beckham was made <u>entirely</u> of chocolate.
   a. partly
   b. carefully
   c. evenly
   d. completely

9. The game is still known as football in most parts of the world <u>besides</u> North America.
   a. except
   b. within
   c. especially
   d. close to

10. <u>Appropriately</u>, the first Women's World Cup was held in China in 1991.
    a. correctly
    b. wrongly
    c. accidentally
    d. happily

WORDS THAT GO TOGETHER

A. Find words in the reading that go together with the words below to make phrases.

1. _____ curriculum
2. sporting _____
3. started _____
4. concentrate _____
5. _____ sports
6. ever _____
7. _____ property

B. Complete the sentences with the phrases from Part A.

1. Games played by groups of people are _____.
2. Something that is owned by the whole population of a city, state, or country is _____.
3. The courses of study offered in a place of education is the _____.
4. If you _____ in a certain manner, you began in that way.
5. A single sports contest among others is a _____.
6. _____ is the time between a point in the past and now.
7. If you _____ something, you keep all your attention on it.

C. Now use the phrases in your own sentences.

Example: *Some people would rather play individual sports than* team sports.

USE

Work with a partner to answer the questions. Use complete sentences.

1. *Ever since* the beginning of the Olympics, what have athletes dreamed of doing?
2. What is a place in your city or town that is *public property*?
3. What is the last *sporting event* that you watched, either on television or in person?
4. In your country, what is the latest fashion *trend*?
5. What are three *team sports* that are played in the summer Olympics?
6. What is something that the law in your country has *banned*?
7. What three areas of study are in most students' *school curriculum*?
8. What are examples of these three types of objects: one made *entirely* of wood, one of glass, and one of metal?

COMPREHENSION

UNDERSTANDING MAIN IDEAS

Look at the reading to find the answers to the following questions.

1. What is paragraph 2 mainly about?

   _____

2. Which sentence contains the main idea of paragraph 3?

   _____

3. Which sentence contains the main idea of paragraph 6?

   _____

4. What importance does Brazil have in the world of football?

   _____

5. What significance does David Beckham have to football fans?

   _____

REMEMBERING DETAILS

Reread the passage and circle the letter of the best answer.

1. Football was introduced to Brazil by _____.
   a. Pelé
   b. Garrincha
   c. Miller
   d. Zico

2. A giant chocolate statue of Beckham was made in _____.
   a. London
   b. Paris
   c. Tokyo
   d. Athens

3. In Britain, several kings banned football because _____.
   a. people were having too much fun
   b. too many people were getting killed and injured
   c. too many shops were being damaged
   d. it nearly started a war

4. The first Women's World Cup was held in _____.
   a. China
   b. Britain
   c. Brazil
   d. Japan

5. The hands-free game rules were established _____.
   a. at Cambridge University
   b. at a school called Rugby
   c. by the FIFA in Paris
   d. by the Football Association of England

6. Football is usually NOT played in _____.
   a. fields
   b. parks
   c. streets
   d. courts

7. The first women football players to be paid as full-time professionals were _____.
   a. French
   b. American
   c. Brazilian
   d. Nigerian

8. In ancient times, the _____ took the game of football to Britain.
   a. Chinese
   b. Japanese
   c. Greeks
   d. Romans

MAKING INFERENCES

Some of the following statements are facts from the reading. Other statements can be inferred, or guessed. Write *F* for each factual statement. Write *I* for of each inference.

_____ 1. At any time during the day or night, someone somewhere in the world is probably playing football.

_____ 2. Britain is the undisputed birthplace of modern football.

_____ 3. Although football was played in British schools in the 1800s, there were no formal rules to the game.

_____ 4. Once game rules were established in Britain, it didn't take long for football to become a favorite sport around the world.

_____ 5. In 1904, seven nations got together in Paris to form an international football association.

_____ 6. Women played football in China as far back as 2,000 years ago.

_____ 7. Football is a good way for the poor in Brazil to improve their lives.

_____ 8. A popular football player can make as much or more money off the field as on it.

_____ 9. Football is not the kind of sport that only appeals to a few people.

_____10. Most people think that football will continue to be the most popular sport in the world.

DISCUSSION

Discuss the answers to these questions with your classmates.

1. Would you rather watch football or play it? Why?
2. Do you think that it's fair that women are paid so much less than men in professional sports? Why or why not?
3. Do you think that professional sports players should advertise products? Why or why not?
4. Do you think professional athletes have a responsibility to be good role models, or examples, for young people? Why or why not? Do you think that today's athletes are good role models?

WRITING

On separate paper, write a paragraph or an essay about one of the following topics:

1. What do you think of the Olympic Games today? Are they good / bad / fair / important?
2. Should professional athletes participate in the Olympics?
3. Do you think the salaries of professional sports players are too high? Why or why not?

GRAMMAR AND PUNCTUATION

 THE DEFINITE ARTICLE: NATIONALITIES AND UNIQUE NOUNS

1. **We can use the definite article *the* + nationality adjectives to mean "the people of a country." This is true for nationality adjectives that end in *–ch*, *–sh*, or *–ese* and function as nouns.**

   *When **the British** played football, it was more like war than a game.*

   The Chinese played football over 2,000 years ago.

   (Note: we also use *the Swiss* to mean the people of Switzerland.)

   With other nationalities, the plural noun ends in *–s*. We do not usually use *the* to talk about the people of these countries. However, we do use *the* when referring to ancient nationalities ending in *–s*.

   ***Brazilians** love football.*

   *The ancient **Greeks** and **Romans** played football.*

Fill in the blanks with *the* or *X* for no definite article.

1. Football was one of _____ first team sports played in _____ Olympics.
2. Some people think football is _____ oldest sport in history.
3. _____ Brazilians have some of _____ FIFA's most talented football players.
4. _____ French and _____ Swiss love football.
5. Today, football is not Japan's most popular sport, although _____ Japanese played it a long time ago.
6. _____ first full-time female professional players were _____ Americans.
7. _____ U.S. women's football team has won three Olympic medals.
8. Most people think Brazil is _____ greatest football-playing country in _____ world.
9. It was _____ Romans who introduced football to _____ British.
10. Brazil is _____ only country that has won _____ World Cup five times, and it also has had some of _____ most famous players.

UNIT 13

How Did Convicts Help Settle Australia?

BEFORE YOU READ

Answer these questions.

1. How many people do you think live in Australia today?
2. What are some famous places in Australia?
3. Would you like to visit Australia? Why or why not?

How Did Convicts Help Settle Australia?

1 The British were not the first Europeans to arrive in Australia. Dutch, Spanish, and Portuguese explorers had passed through the vast continent before them without giving it much notice. When an Englishman, Dampier, did land in what is today New South Wales, he **condemned** the land as barren and useless. Then the British explorer Captain James Cook proved his **predecessor** wrong. He landed at Botany Bay in New South Wales in 1770, and with his botanist, Joseph Banks, he proved that the eastern shores were rich and fertile. Although Captain Cook gave an excellent report on all the land he had seen in Australia, the British government made no effort to form a settlement there for several years.

2 For many years it was the **policy** of the British government to send men and women found guilty of **breaking the law** to America. There, as punishment, these prisoners were forced to work on big farms until they had **served out their sentences**, and they were then **set free**. This policy of sending criminals abroad was called "transportation."

3 However, all this changed with the loss of the American colonies. In 1776, the American colonies declared their independence from Britain. When they became the United States of America, no more **convicts** could be sent there. The British government was in a difficult position. People were still being sentenced to transportation, but there was nowhere to send them. Soon, the jails were overcrowded.

4 Joseph Banks, Captain Cook's botanist, suggested New South Wales as a good place for a convict settlement. "The soil is good there," he said, "and soon they will grow all their own food." Lord Sydney—after whom the capital of Australia is named—had the **task** of looking after the British colonies. He decided to try Banks' plan. He selected Captain Arthur Phillip, a naval officer, to take charge of the new settlement.

5 In May 1787, the First Fleet, consisting of eleven ships, left England for New South Wales. **On board** were about 1,400 people, of whom 780 were convicts. The rest were mainly soldiers to guard the convicts and seamen to work on the ships. About 20 percent of the convicts were women; the oldest convict was eighty-two, and the youngest one was about ten years old. The voyage to Australia was very slow. It took eight months; six of these were spent at sea, and two were spent in ports to get supplies. The fleet finally arrived in Botany Bay in 1788. Two more

convict fleets arrived in 1790 and 1791, and ships continued to come to other ports in Australia for over seventy years.

6 A major problem of the convict system was the **severity** of its punishments. Among the convicts on the First Fleet was a woman who was transported for stealing a coat. The British also transported a man who had received a sentence of fourteen years for killing a rabbit on his master's property. Others were transported only because they supported different political opinions. There were many real criminals who were transported as well, but by today's standards many of the convicts would not be considered criminals.

7 Conditions on the ships were **deplorable**. Ship owners were paid "per head," or for each person they transported. To make as much money as possible, the owners overcrowded the ships. The convicts were chained below deck, where there was no sunlight or fresh air. They suffered a lot, and many died on the way. Because so many died on the ships, later the government paid a bonus to ship owners whose passengers had arrived **safe and sound** at the end of the journey.

8 For convicts who **made it** to Australia, conditions were a little better. Those who were well behaved were **assigned to** settlers as workers or servants, and if they worked for good people, they served out their sentences under pleasant conditions. Other convicts worked in groups for the government. They did various kinds of jobs, such as clearing land, making roads and bridges, and constructing public buildings. Those convicts who refused to work or tried to escape were severely punished.

9 Convicts could win their freedom back more quickly with good behavior. They could qualify for a "Ticket of Leave" or a "Certificate of Freedom." Convicts who got their freedom were allowed to move around the country and work in any kind of profession they liked. Soon, many educated ex-convicts became lawyers, teachers, and business owners. Others bought land and became rich settlers.

10 Convicts were not the only settlers in the country; free settlers had been coming from Britain and starting farms since 1793. In the beginning, the convicts were a great help to the new settlers. But later, when the number of free settlers grew, they objected to the transportation of convicts. They thought it was unfair that their new land was filled with criminals. By 1840, objection was so strong that no more convicts were transported to the mainland. Instead, they were sent *from* there to Tasmania, an island south of Australia.

11 Convicts had never been sent to western Australia, but in the middle of the nineteenth century, the colony there suddenly asked for them. There was a shortage of **labor** in the region, and the colony could only progress with convict labor. Britain supplied the colony with convicts starting in 1850 and ending in 1868, and the convicts helped build it up by constructing roads, bridges, and public buildings.

12 A total of 162,000 men and women—transported on 806 ships—came as convicts to Australia. By the time the British policy of transportation ended, the population of Australia had increased to over a million. Without the convicts' hard work, first as servants and later as settlers, it wouldn't have been possible for the government and the free settlers to create a nation. The transportation of convicts is an essential part of Australia's history. Today, many Australians **acknowledge** their convict ancestors and are **grateful** for their contributions to the country.

VOCABULARY

MEANING

Circle the letter of the answer that is closest in meaning to the underlined word.

1. No more <u>convicts</u> could be sent to the American colonies.
    a. colonists
    b. prisoners
    c. soldiers
    d. government officials

2. Conditions on the ships were <u>deplorable</u>.
    a. enjoyable
    b. terrible
    c. surprising
    d. depressing

3. There was a shortage of <u>labor</u> in the region.
    a. farmers
    b. settlers
    c. workers
    d. business owners

4. Many Australians are <u>grateful</u> for the contributions of their convict ancestors.
   a. thankful
   b. ashamed
   c. lucky
   d. punished

5. He <u>condemned</u> the land as barren and useless.
   a. described
   b. disapproved of
   c. announced
   d. gave a name to

6. Today, many Australians <u>acknowledge</u> their convict ancestors.
   a. try to hide the facts about
   b. remember the details of
   c. admit the truth about
   d. tell a story about

7. It was the <u>policy</u> of the British government to send men and women found guilty of breaking the law to America.
   a. law
   b. problem
   c. demand
   d. idea

8. A major problem of the convict system was the <u>severity</u> of its punishments.
   a. lightness
   b. strangeness
   c. popularity
   d. seriousness

9. Captain James Cook proved his <u>predecessor</u> wrong.
   a. someone who came before
   b. someone who left after
   c. someone who arrived at the same time
   d. someone who would come in the future

10. Lord Sydney had the <u>task</u> of looking after the British colonies.
    a. thought
    b. plan
    c. job
    d. choice

WORDS THAT GO TOGETHER

A. Find words in the reading that go together with the words below to make phrases.

1. _____ board
2. made _____
3. served _____ their _____
4. _____ and sound
5. assigned _____
6. _____ the law
7. _____ free

B. Complete the sentences with the phrases from Part A.

1. Convicts who have completed all the time of their punishments in jail have _____.
2. When a person or thing is _____ someone, it is given to him or her to use.
3. People who are riding on a bus, train, plane, or ship are _____ that form of transportation.
4. People who are _____ are allowed to go out and act as they want, and are no longer under someone else's control.
5. If you are _____, you are alive, not in danger, and in good health.
6. If you arrive somewhere, you can say that you have _____ there.
7. If you do something that is not legal, you are _____.

C. Now use the phrases in your own sentences.

Example: *The search party looked for the hiker, and after two days, they found him safe and sound.*

Work with a partner to answer the questions. Use complete sentences.

1. What is a *policy* in your school or workplace that you don't agree with? Explain why.

2. What is a *task* that you must do at work or home?

3. What is a place that has *deplorable* conditions? Describe it.

4. If you could be *on board* any form of transportation right now, how would you like to be traveling? Where would you be going?

5. What is something that you are *grateful* for?

6. What are three types of *labor* that are important to your country's economy?

7. If you were suddenly *set free* from your school, job, and other obligations, what is the first thing you would do?

8. What are two things that people are often afraid to *acknowledge*?

COMPREHENSION

UNDERSTANDING MAIN IDEAS

Circle the letter of the best answer.

1. The main idea of paragraph 1 is that _____.

   a. the English explorer Dampier condemned New South Wales as a barren and useless land

   b. the British government formed a settlement many years after Captain Cook arrived in Australia

   c. explorers from many countries visited Australia before the British finally started a settlement there

   d. Captain Cook and his botanist, Joseph Banks, proved that the eastern shores of New South Wales were rich and fertile

2. The main idea of paragraph 5 is that _____.

   a. on board the First Fleet were about 1,400 people, of whom 780 were convicts

   b. of the eight months it took the First Fleet to get to Australia, six were spent at sea and two at port getting supplies

c. about 20 percent of the convicts were women; the oldest convict was eighty-two, and the youngest about ten

d. over seventy years of convict transport began in 1787, when the First Fleet of convicts, soldiers, and seamen sailed to Australia

3. The main idea of paragraph 10 is that _____.
   a. the first free settlers came in 1793 and started farms
   b. in the beginning, the convicts were a great help to the free settlers
   c. free settlers finally stopped the transportation of convicts to Australia
   d. after 1840, convicts were transported to the island of Tasmania

4. The main idea of the last paragraph is that _____.
   a. a total of 162,000 men and women—transported on 806 ships—came as convicts to Australia
   b. today many Australians acknowledge their convict ancestors
   c. by the time the British policy of transportation ended, the population of Australia had grown to over a million
   d. the convicts played an important part in the history of Australia

REMEMBERING DETAILS

Reread the passage and answer the questions. Write complete sentences.

1. Why was one of the convicts on the First Fleet given a sentence of fourteen years?

   _____

2. Why did the free settlers object to the transportation of convicts?

   _____

3. When and where did Captain James Cook arrive in Australia?

   _____

4. Who was the first British official to decide to send convicts to Australia?

   _____

5. Why did many of the convicts suffer and die on the first voyages to Australia?

   _____

6. How many ships were in the First Fleet?

_____

7. What are three jobs that the convicts did for the government in Australia?

_____

8. When did the last shipment of convicts arrive in Australia?

_____

MAKING INFERENCES

Some of the following statements are facts from the reading. Other statements can be inferred, or guessed. Write _F_ for each factual statement. Write _I_ for each inference.

_____ 1. Even though Cook told the British government how good the land was, they didn't make any effort to settle Australia for several years.

_____ 2. For many years, it was the policy of the British government to transport criminals to America.

_____ 3. The convict settlement of Australia probably wouldn't have happened if the American colonies hadn't declared their independence.

_____ 4. Though the voyage was extremely difficult, the convicts were better off in Australia than in England's crowded jails.

_____ 5. In the eighteenth and nineteenth centuries, the British system of justice was not very fair or merciful.

_____ 6. Ship owners were paid "per head," or for each person they transported.

_____ 7. The ship owners had little caring or compassion for the convicts.

_____ 8. As the number of free settlers grew, they objected to having convicts in their new land.

_____ 9. The convicts had valuable skills and knowledge.

_____10. In western Australia, the convicts constructed roads, bridges, and public buildings.

DISCUSSION

Discuss the answers to these questions with your classmates.

1. What do you think about the British sending their convicts to Australia? Would this type of "transportation system" work today? Why or why not?
2. Do you think convicts today should do hard work like building roads, cleaning highways, and so on?
3. Is your country an "old" country or a "new" country? What are the advantages and disadvantages of living in an ancient land? In a new land?
4. Would you like to explore a new country? Why or why not?

WRITING

On separate paper, write a paragraph or an essay about one of the following topics:

1. What are some problems you may encounter when you live in a new country?
2. Describe or explain the fairness of the justice system in relation to some crimes we hear about in the news. Are court decisions generally fair or unfair?
3. What should the punishment be for minor crimes (such as driving too fast or taking something from a supermarket without paying)?

GRAMMAR AND PUNCTUATION

THE PAST PERFECT

> **To form the past perfect, we use _had_ + the past participle of the verb. Notice the past perfect verb in the second sentence below.**
>
> _The British were not the first Europeans to arrive in Australia. Dutch, Spanish, and Portuguese explorers_ **had passed** _through the vast continent before them without giving it much notice._
>
> **_Had passed_ is the past perfect of the verb _pass_. The past perfect shows that something happened before another past event or time. In this case, first the Dutch, Spanish, and Portuguese passed through the continent. Then the British arrived in Australia.**

Read the sentences from the reading. Identify the order of events. Write *1* for the first event and *2* for the second event.

1. Although Cook gave an excellent report on all the land he had seen in Australia, the British government made no effort to form a settlement there for several years.

   _____ Cook gave an excellent report.

   _____ Cook saw all the land.

2. These convicts were forced to work on big farms until they had served out their sentences, and they were then set free.

   _____ Convicts served their sentences.

   _____ Convicts were set free.

3. Banks, a colleague of Cook who had been with him to Australia, suggested New South Wales as a good place for a convict settlement.

   _____ Banks suggested New South Wales as a convict settlement.

   _____ Banks was in Australia with Cook.

4. The British also transported a man who had received a sentence of fourteen years for killing a rabbit on his master's property.

   _____ The man received a sentence of fourteen years.

   _____ The British transported the man.

5. Because so many died on the ships, later the government paid a bonus to ship owners whose passengers had arrived safe and sound at the end of the journey.

   _____ The passengers arrived safe and sound.

   _____ The government paid a bonus to ship owners.

6. By the time the British policy of transportation ended, the population of Australia had increased to over a million.

   _____ The policy of transportation ended.

   _____ The population increased to over a million.

UNIT 14

How Do Greetings Differ Around the World?

BEFORE YOU READ

Answer these questions.

1. How do you greet a friend or relative?
2. How do you greet a stranger?
3. What greeting customs do you know from other countries?

How Do Greetings Differ Around the World?

1 There is a range of different greetings around the world, from a simple "hello," a handshake, a kiss, or a **bow**, to sticking out your tongue in Tibet! But how you shake someone's hand in one country may differ from the custom in another. In some countries you kiss as a greeting, but how many times do you kiss? Which cheek do you start with? In which countries do you bow? Here are some examples of greetings from a few parts of the world.

2 A bow or a light handshake with eyes **averted** is the usual greeting in most Asian cultures where people do not like to have body contact when greeting. In China and Taiwan, shaking hands is customary, but people often **nod their heads** or give a slight bow as well. The Chinese like to **applaud**, and a visitor may be greeted with a group of people clapping their hands. When you are applauded, you must return the applause or say thank you.

3 In Japan, a graceful bow is the traditional greeting. The Japanese have also adopted the Western handshake, but the handshake is light, with eyes averted. When being introduced, visitors can make a slight bow to show respect for Japanese customs. In Korea, as in Japan, the bow is the traditional form of greeting. For men, a handshake sometimes follows the bow. Women do not shake hands with men; they usually just nod.

4 People in the Philippines are much more touch-oriented than those in other Asian cultures. Here, handshaking is a common custom, with both men and women shaking hands in a friendly fashion. Filipinos may also greet each other with a quick **flick of the eyebrows**.

5 In Malaysia, people greet each other saying, "Where are you going?" But this is not really a question. The polite answer is, "Just for a walk." In India, people greet each other with "Namaste." As they say this, they bend or nod and put their **palms** together as though they are praying.

6 European greetings vary from shaking hands to kissing. In Britain, people do not like physical contact very much, so they **opt for** the handshake. Between friends they just say, "Hi!" or "How are you?" However, you are not **supposed to** say how you really are. Between close friends and family, kissing is normal. Germany follows the same rules as Britain. In France, however, kissing is the rule. Multiple kisses are normal and will vary from region to region. In most places, a two-kiss greeting is polite, but in Paris, the greeting is four kisses, starting with the

left cheek. In Brittany, there is a three-kiss greeting, and in most other parts of France it is a two-kiss greeting. The exception is the south of France, where sometimes five kisses are not unusual. In the Netherlands, three kisses are expected, and you always start and finish kissing on the right cheek. If you're greeting a very close friend or an older person, four or five kisses are normal. In Spain, Austria, and Scandinavia, there is a two-kiss ritual. In Spain, you always begin with the right cheek. In Belgium, it's one kiss for a person about the same age as you, but three kisses to show respect for a person who is more than ten years older than you. Many may think that Italians would do a lot of kissing as a form of greeting, but the usual greeting there is a handshake. For friends, handshakes and hugs are **the norm**. Kissing is **restricted to** very close friends and family, and there are no special rules as to which cheek to kiss first.

7 Americans shake hands, using a **firm grip**. They are taught to do this to show honesty. They also look someone in the eye when they greet them, to show they are not shy or weak. Americans also say, "Hi!" or "How are you doing?" As in Britain, they don't really expect you to answer that question. Hugs are used among close friends, though there are variations depending on where in the United States people live.

8 Handshakes are important in the Middle East and can be quite long. Most Arabs shake hands every time they meet someone and every time they leave. This applies wherever they meet—in the street, at home, or in the office. In Saudi Arabia, they shake hands on meeting, talk for a while, and then shake hands again. This can happen ten times a day with the same person. Arabs will kiss and hug friends of the same sex as a form of greeting, and they also look the person in the eye.

9 Greetings in Senegal take the form of handshakes, and they are even more significant there. In Senegal, a person will stop doing something really important to spend ten minutes greeting a person that he or she has seen an hour ago. This is to acknowledge the existence of another human being and is seen as a **priority** in Senegalese culture. Every member of the community greets every other member, regardless of status or wealth. They must greet each other even if one of them is in the middle of a **business transaction** or is discussing something with someone else. In the greeting, they repeat the other person's family name over and over to acknowledge that person's entire family, both living and dead. The Senegalese are **offended** if you do not greet them first before asking a simple question. For example, if you ask, "Where did he go?" without

offering a greeting first, you may get a response such as, "He went to learn how to greet." This is another way of saying that you are rude.

10 There are many variations in South American countries, but the general rule is a handshake at first meeting and a kiss on the cheek between close friends. Men often **embrace** if they know each other well. Strangers do not address each other by their first names when they are being introduced. Their title (Mr., Mrs.), followed by their first name, is a common greeting, because it indicates friendship and respect. Eye contact is essential in South America.

11 Some cultures have variations on these common greetings. For example, the Inuit of North America traditionally used the *kunik* in place of the kiss. The kunik involves placing noses next to each other and lightly rubbing or **sniffing**. Most Inuit now use their lips to kiss, but the kunik is sometimes still used with children. Though most New Zealanders use a handshake when greeting, the tradition of the native Maori people is to press noses together to show trust and closeness.

12 In many Asian countries, people like to exchange business cards when they first meet, but they have special customs for doing this. To show respect for the other person, they use both hands when giving and taking a card, and they take time to study the other person's card before putting it away. They also never write on someone else's card.

13 Of course, these are only a few of the greetings used around the world. There are even more variations in other countries. Learning about these customs not only makes us more polite travelers, but also gives us **insight** into the differences between people around the world, as well as an understanding of each country's special values.

VOCABULARY

MEANING

Circle the letter of the answer that is closest in meaning to the underlined word.

1. The Chinese like to <u>applaud</u>.
   a. call out loudly
   b. wave the arms
   c. strike the hands together
   d. move the head up and down

2. The Senegalese are <u>offended</u> if you don't greet them.
   a. afraid
   b. rude
   c. confused
   d. upset

3. It involves placing noses next to each other and lightly <u>sniffing</u>.
   a. blowing air out of the mouth
   b. blowing air out of the nose
   c. breathing air into the nose
   d. touching with a light kiss

4. The usual greeting is a light handshake with eyes <u>averted</u>.
   a. looking straight ahead
   b. turned away
   c. looking up
   d. closed

5. As they say this, they bend or nod and put their <u>palms</u> together.
   a. fingers
   b. back of the hands
   c. front of the arms
   d. inside of the hands

6. Learning about these customs can give us <u>insight</u> into the differences between people around the world.
   a. understanding of
   b. opinions about
   c. sorrow for
   d. love for

7. There is a range of different greetings, including a simple handshake, a kiss, or a <u>bow</u>.

    a. bending forward of the body

    b. turning of the body

    c. kneeling on the ground

    d. raising of the arms

8. Men often <u>embrace</u> if they know each other well.

    a. kiss each other on the cheek

    b. pat each other on the back

    c. hold each other's hands and shake firmly

    d. put their arms around each other

9. This is seen as a <u>priority</u> in Senegalese culture.

    a. of great interest

    b. first in importance

    c. a cause of joy

    d. a reason to act

WORDS THAT GO TOGETHER

A. Find words in the reading that go together with the words below to make phrases.

1. _____ norm

2. _____ their heads

3. opt _____

4. _____ grip

5. business _____

6. _____ of the _____

7. supposed _____

8. restricted _____

B. Complete the sentences with the phrases from Part A.

1. If you make a _____, you perform a trade, purchase, sale, or other type of money- or business-related activity.
2. If people _____, they bend their heads forward and down as a sign of greeting or agreement.
3. If you are _____ do something, you are expected to do it because of duty, law, or custom.
4. Usual or expected behavior is _____.
5. If you _____ something, you choose it.
6. A _____ is a quick movement up and down of the line of hair above the eyes.
7. When something is done only for a certain purpose or used for only a particular group, it is _____ that purpose or group.
8. When you have a very tight hold on something, you have a _____ on it.

C. Now use the phrases in your own sentences.

Example: *I was* supposed to *be at work early, but I slept late.*

 USE

Work with a partner to answer the questions. Use complete sentences.

1. What is a *priority* in your life now?
2. In your culture, what does it mean when people *nod their heads*?
3. What is one common *business transaction* that people make?
4. Where can you see people *applaud*?
5. When would you want to have a *firm grip* on something?
6. What behavior or clothing is *restricted to* a certain group in your culture?
7. In your culture, what are you *supposed to* do if a teacher enters the room?
8. What is *the norm* when you get together with friends after work or school?

COMPREHENSION

UNDERSTANDING MAIN IDEAS

Some of the following statements are main ideas, and some are supporting statements. Some of them are stated directly in the reading. Find the statements. Write *M* for each main idea. Write *S* for each supporting statement.

_____ 1. There is a range of different greetings around the world.

_____ 2. European greetings vary from shaking hands to kissing.

_____ 3. In Belgium, it's one kiss for a person about the same age as you, but three kisses to show respect for a person who is more than ten years older.

_____ 4. In many Asian countries, people like to exchange business cards when they first meet, but they have special customs for doing this.

_____ 5. To show respect for the other person, they use both hands when giving and taking a card, and they take time to study the other person's card before putting it away.

REMEMBERING DETAILS

Reread the passage and answer the questions. Write complete sentences.

1. Why do Americans look people in the eye when they greet them?

   _____

2. What is the usual greeting in most Asian cultures?

   _____

3. Why do the Senegalese repeat a person's family name when they are greeting him or her?

   _____

4. What is the traditional greeting in Japan?

   _____

5. What does the kunik greeting of the Inuit people involve?

   _____

6. When you are applauded by a group of Chinese, what must you do?

   _____

7. When do most Arabs shake hands?

    _____

8. What is the kissing custom in the Netherlands?

    _____

MAKING INFERENCES

Some of the following statements can be inferred, or guessed, from the reading and others cannot. Circle the number of each statement that can be inferred.

1. A Japanese man would not be comfortable if someone greeted him with an embrace.
2. In India, you don't see people kissing or embracing when they meet.
3. In Europe, people don't like to shake hands very much.
4. In some cultures, people ask questions when they greet because they want to know more about each other.
5. An American would probably not trust someone who gave a weak handshake with eyes averted.
6. If you were talking with a man from Senegal, it would be neither unusual nor impolite for him to interrupt your conversation several times.
7. South Americans don't know about the greeting customs of Europeans.
8. If you don't know the greeting customs of a country in which you are traveling, you might do something that people think is very rude.

DISCUSSION

Discuss the answers to these questions with your classmates.

1. What do greetings tell us about a culture?
2. Why is it important for people to learn the customs and values of people in other countries?
3. In some cultures, people spend a lot of time and use "small talk" (casual conversation about the weather, family members, etc.) when greeting others. In other cultures, time is very valuable, and people eliminate small talk. Which style do you prefer? Why?
4. When do you use small talk in your culture?

WRITING

On separate paper, write a paragraph or an essay about one of the following topics:

1. When and how do you greet and say farewell in your culture?
2. How and when do you give gifts in your culture?
3. To whom do you show respect in your culture? How do you show respect?

GRAMMAR AND PUNCTUATION

 ## FORMS OF *OTHER*

We use forms of *other* as adjectives or pronouns to mean "more things or people of the same kind."

- *Another* means one more in addition to the one we already have talked about.

  *How you shake someone's hand in one country may differ from a custom in **another**.* (= one more country)

- *Other* or *others* (without *the*) means several more in addition to the one(s) we already talked about.

  *Filipinos are more touch-oriented than **other** Asian cultures.*

  *Of the Asian peoples, Filipinos are more touch-oriented than **others**.*

- *The other* or *the others* means all that is remaining from a specific group. (Note: *the others* is often used with *all* or *all of*.)

  *There are two forms of greeting in Asia: one is the bow and **the other** is a light handshake.*

  *In Senegal, the custom of greeting is more important than **all the others**.*

- *Each other* and *one another* are reciprocal pronouns. *Each other* usually refers to two subjects and *one another* to more than two; however, we use either of the two forms in informal English.

  *In India, people greet **each other** with "Namaste."*

  *In Britain, a group of friends might greet **one another** with a simple "Hi!"*

Complete the sentences with a form of *other* from the list below. You may use the words more than once.

another	other	others	the other	the others	each other

1. In Spain, it's a two-kiss greeting. You kiss one cheek and then
   _____.

2. In some countries, they kiss; in _____ they shake hands.

3. Americans look _____ in the eyes when they shake hands.

4. In some parts of France, they have a two-kiss greeting, in
   _____ they may have a four-kiss greeting.

5. I kissed my friend twice when I saw her, but she was expecting
   _____, as three kisses is the custom in that part of the
   country.

6. In some Asian countries, two people bow to _____. In
   _____ countries in Asia, they give a light handshake.

7. France is the only European country which has up to a five-kiss greeting;
   all _____ have only a two- or three-kiss greeting.

8. In Korea, sometimes men have two forms of greeting, one after
   _____. First, it's a handshake and then a bow.

9. In Senegal, it is disrespectful not to acknowledge the existence of
   _____ human being.

10. In Britain, one friend may greet you with, "How are you?" and
    _____ with, "Hi!"

UNIT 15

Why Is Napoleon Famous?

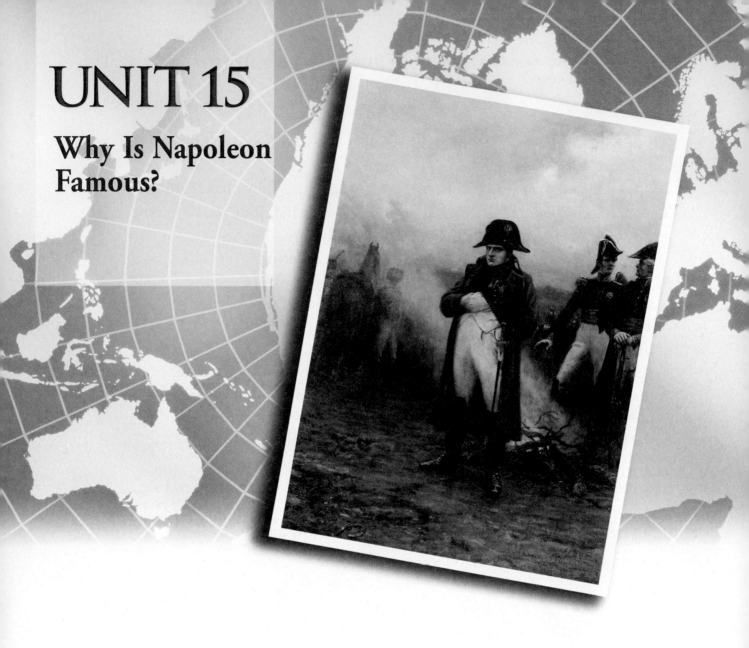

BEFORE YOU READ

Answer these questions.

1. Who was a great leader of your country?
2. Who are some famous world leaders of the past?
3. Who are some famous world leaders of the present?

Why Is Napoleon Famous?

1 Many portraits of Napoleon show him with his right hand placed inside his coat or shirt. In fact, there was nothing wrong with Napoleon's hand. At the time, portrait painters thought this **pose** made men look more **dignified**. Also, they had one less hand to draw and paint. Looking at his portraits, we can tell that Napoleon was an important person. But who was this man?

2 Napoleon Bonaparte was born in 1769 on the French island of Corsica, not far from the coast of Italy. He was one of fourteen children. As a boy, Napoleon loved to play soldiers with his brothers. When he was old enough, his parents sent him to military school to learn how to become a real soldier. After he completed his training at the military school, Napoleon became an officer in the French army.

3 Four years later, in 1789, there was a sudden and violent change in France. Tired of paying heavy taxes so the king and his nobles could live in luxury, poor and middle-class people started a revolution. They executed the king and queen and many of their royal friends and then **declared** France a republic where all people were to pay taxes according to their wealth.

4 When the rulers of other European countries heard what happened in France, they thought they, too, would **lose control** over their countries. Austria and Britain **went to war with** the new republic of France. Napoleon was a brilliant officer and was only twenty-seven years old when he was made Commander-in-Chief of the French army in Italy. He won one victory after another, **defeating** the Austrians in eighteen battles. Then he moved his army to Egypt to stop the British trade route to India. He **won a victory** over the Egyptians in 1798 at the Battle of the Pyramids. In 1799, his troops in Egypt discovered the Rosetta stone, an important object which helped people to understand ancient Egyptian writing for the first time. Napoleon had with him scholars from many **fields** who wanted to set up schools in Egypt. One group of scholars studied the pyramids and started the science of Egyptology. However, the British destroyed Napoleon's ships and he lost the Rosetta stone to them. Then Napoleon decided to return to France.

5 When Napoleon returned to France, he was appointed first consul. The French needed a strong ruler at this time, and Napoleon was one. He became consul for life in 1802, and in 1804, Napoleon declared himself

emperor of France. The Pope came from Rome to **perform the ceremony**. Napoleon, richly dressed, listened to the service. Then Napoleon took the crown before the Pope could take it, and he put it on his own head. He did this to show that he got the crown because of his **wisdom** and military skill; he was not simply given the honor by the Pope.

6 Soon afterward, Napoleon made himself master of almost all of Europe. He **conquered** Austria in 1805 and Prussia in 1806. Then he formed an alliance with Russia, and he made one of his brothers the king of Spain and another brother king of Holland.

7 In France, he ruled wisely and well, and he restored **law and order** after the revolution. He reorganized the French government and the Bank of France. He built many fine roads and improved the old ones. He turned Paris into a beautiful city with wide streets, fine bridges, and beautiful buildings and monuments, such as the Arc de Triomphe. More important still, he improved the laws. To this day, his Napoleonic Code is the **foundation** of European law, as well as of laws in Central and South America and Quebec in Canada. Napoleon wrote the Code's original 2,281 articles himself, although he was completely self-taught in legal matters. The Code created a legal system in which all citizens were equal. It was so clearly written that it could be read and understood by ordinary people at a time when all laws were written in Latin and understood by only a few.

8 Napoleon was a genius as an army commander. He conquered the huge Austrian Empire and ruled Italy, Switzerland, and Germany. He had the largest empire seen in Europe since the days of the ancient Romans. The only country he could not defeat was Britain, losing to the British in 1805 in the Battle of Trafalgar. Then, in 1812, Napoleon made his biggest mistake by invading Russia. He entered Moscow, but he found that nearly all the people had left. There were fires all over the city, and most of it was destroyed. With no place to house his soldiers and no food for them to eat in the **bitter** Russian winter, Napoleon **had no choice but to** retreat. Napoleon lost half a million men in Russia. When he was finally defeated, he was sent to the island of Elba in the Mediterranean. By 1814, one million Frenchmen were dead. Napoleon was **humiliated**.

9 After ten months in Elba, Napoleon escaped, went back to France, and declared himself emperor again. He ruled for 100 days. In the meantime, the Europeans gathered their armies to end his rule. The combined armies, led by the British Duke of Wellington, defeated Napoleon at Waterloo in 1815. After this, he was sent to the island of St.

Helena in the Atlantic Ocean, where he died six years later at age fifty-two. We do not know what Napoleon died of exactly. Some doctors argued that he died of cancer; others say he was poisoned.

10 Napoleon was a military genius and had a brilliant mind. He fought many wars and thought there would not be peace in Europe until the continent was under one ruler—himself. Perhaps Napoleon would have been an even greater ruler had he not been **driven by** his love of power.

VOCABULARY

MEANING

Circle the letter of the answer that is closest in meaning to the underlined word.

1. His Napoleonic code is the <u>foundation</u> of European law.
   a. history
   b. basis
   c. explanation
   d. truth

2. Napoleon had with him scholars from many <u>fields</u>.
   a. places of birth
   b. kinds of schools
   c. areas of knowledge
   d. types of governments

3. There was no place to house his soldiers in the <u>bitter</u> Russian winter.
   a. long
   b. cold
   c. dark
   d. empty

4. He won one victory after another, <u>defeating</u> the Austrians in eighteen battles.
   a. joining
   b. tricking
   c. directing
   d. beating

5. Many portraits of Napoleon show him in a <u>pose</u> with his right hand placed inside his coat.
   a. outfit
   b. hairstyle
   c. position
   d. movement

6. Napoleon was <u>humiliated</u> when he was defeated.
   a. shamed
   b. punished
   c. praised
   d. tortured

7. He got the crown because of his own <u>wisdom</u> and military skill.
   a. strength
   b. courage
   c. knowledge
   d. talent

8. Portrait painters thought this pose made men look more <u>dignified</u>.
   a. handsome
   b. young
   c. serious
   d. intelligent

9. They <u>declared</u> France a republic.
   a. officially stated
   b. informally decided
   c. put into writing
   d. voted into law

10. Napoleon <u>conquered</u> Austria in 1805.
    a. went to live in
    b. tried to control
    c. set free
    d. took control of by force

WORDS THAT GO TOGETHER

A. Find words in the reading that go together with the words below to make phrases.

1. _____ control
2. _____ the ceremony
3. had _____ choice _____ to
4. law and _____
5. _____ to war with
6. _____ a victory
7. driven _____

B. Complete the sentences with the phrases from Part A.

1. When people _____, they do certain actions that are the custom at an important public, social, or religious occasion.

2. If a country _____ another country, there would be fighting between the two nations.

3. If you were forced to do something even though you didn't really want to do it, then you _____ do that unwanted action.

4. If you have a forceful quality of mind or spirit that makes you get things done or perform certain actions, then you are _____ that force.

5. When you _____ of something, you no longer have power or command over it.

6. To have succeeded in a war or any kind of struggle is to have

   _____.

7. When the people are governed and controlled, there is

   _____ in that place.

C. Now use the phrases in your own sentences.

Example: *The young woman was* driven by *a strong desire to succeed in business.*

USE

Work with a partner to answer the questions. Use complete sentences.

1. How do people behave when they *lose control*? Name two things they do.
2. What *fields* of study interest you the most?

3. Why is it important to have *law and order* in a society?

4. What are some characteristics of a *dignified* person?

5. What conditions might exist in a *bitter* winter?

6. What are two countries that *went to war with* each other?

7. What is a typical *pose* of a fashion model? A world leader? A rock star?

8. Was there ever a time when you *had no choice but to* do something you really didn't want to do? Explain the situation.

COMPREHENSION

UNDERSTANDING MAIN IDEAS

Look at the reading to find the answers to the following questions.

1. What is the main idea of paragraph 3?

   _____

2. Which sentence contains the main idea of paragraph 6?

   _____

3. How did Napoleon rule France wisely and well?

   _____

4. How did the Europeans finally defeat Napoleon?

   _____

REMEMBERING DETAILS

Reread the passage and circle the letter of the best answer.

1. In 1804, Napoleon declared himself _____.
   a. first consul
   b. emperor of France
   c. consul for life
   d. emperor for life

2. The only country that Napoleon could not defeat was _____.
   a. Italy
   b. Britain
   c. Switzerland
   d. Germany

3. In 1789, the _____ started a revolution in France.
   a. king and his nobles
   b. French army led by Napoleon
   c. poor and middle-class people
   d. Austrian Empire

4. The Napoleonic Code is the foundation for laws in _____.
   a. Europe
   b. the United States
   c. Asian countries
   d. Russia

5. Napoleon was born _____.
   a. on the coast of Italy
   b. in Paris
   c. on Corsica
   d. in Austria

6. The Napoleonic Code created a legal system in which _____.
   a. the king and his nobles were not taxed
   b. the army ruled by force
   c. the country was divided into upper and lower classes
   d. all citizens were equal

7. At age fifty-two, Napoleon died _____.
   a. at Waterloo
   b. on the island of Elba
   c. in the Battle of Trafalgar
   d. on the island of St. Helena

8. Napoleon moved his army to Egypt to _____.

   a. stop the British trade route to India

   b. find the Rosetta stone

   c. bring scholars to set up schools

   d. defeat the Austrians

 MAKING INFERENCES

Some of the following statements can be inferred, or guessed, from the reading and others cannot. Circle the number of each statement that can be inferred.

1. The Russians burned Moscow as part of their strategy to defeat Napoleon.

2. Napoleon did not like the Pope.

3. Napoleon believed that all people should understand their laws.

4. If Napoleon had not been defeated at Waterloo, he would have ruled France for at least another twenty years.

5. Napoleon was a brilliant leader who believed in equality and justice for everyone.

6. Napoleon believed that under his rule, all of Europe would be at peace.

7. The scholars that Napoleon brought with him to Egypt failed to do any work there.

8. When Napoleon was young, he wasn't interested in becoming a soldier.

DISCUSSION

Discuss the answers to these questions with your classmates.

1. What are the qualities of a great leader?

2. What has led to the defeat of great leaders and countries in the past?

3. Name at least three types of governments. What are the good points and bad points of each type?

4. If you could be the leader of your country, what changes would you make?

WRITING

On separate paper, write a paragraph or an essay about one of the following topics:

1. Describe one or two of your best qualities. Give examples.
2. Write a definition of love. Describe two types of love, such as love of power or love of money.
3. What is your goal or ambition in life? How are you going to achieve it?

GRAMMAR AND PUNCTUATION

PARALLEL STRUCTURE

We use conjunctions such as *and, but,* and *or* to connect words or phrases. The words before and after these conjunctions must have the same grammatical form. This means there is parallel structure.

*Napoleon's right hand was placed in his **coat** or **shirt**.* (nouns)

*The revolution was **sudden** and **violent**.* (adjectives)

*He ruled **wisely** and **well**.* (adverbs)

*He **entered** Moscow, but he **found** that the people had left.* (verbs)

Rewrite the incorrect sentences with correct parallel structure. Use correct word forms.

1. Napoleon had military skill and wise.

    _____

2. The poor people of France paid high taxes and starving.

    _____

3. They started a revolution and executing the king and queen.

    _____

4. After the revolution, Napoleon restored law and orderly.

    _____

5. He reorganized the French government and build many roads.

    _____

6. Napoleon lost his shipping and the Rosetta stone to the British.

_____

7. Napoleon took his army to Egypt, but he also took men of learning and scientific.

_____

8. When Napoleon entered Moscow it was a cold and emptiness city.

_____

9. Napoleon was powerful and brilliantly.

_____

10. Napoleon is responsible for the wide boulevards, the beautiful buildings, and the monumental in Paris today.

_____

UNIT 16

Who Invented the World Wide Web?

BEFORE YOU READ

Answer these questions.

1. Do you use a computer? If so, what do you mostly use it for?
2. What are the Internet and the World Wide Web used for?
3. How important are computers in society today? Why?

Who Invented the World Wide Web?

1 Tim Berners-Lee is not a **household name** like Bill Gates. He is not **outrageously** rich or famous. He could have been, but he didn't want to be. Tim Berners-Lee is a quiet man who does not like the **spotlight**. He is the man who invented the World Wide Web and revolutionized the Internet. Berners-Lee's invention permits anyone with a computer to easily access a vast amount of information on any subject. This is a great **contribution to** the use of computers and to society. Some people believe it is as important as Gutenberg's printing press.

2 Tim Berners-Lee was born in London, England, in 1955. He grew up in a family that talked a lot about computers and math, since both of his parents were computer scientists who worked on the design of the first commercial computer. As a small child, he made computers out of cardboard boxes. Later, when he attended Oxford University to study physics, he made his first real computer. He constructed it out of various parts of a machine and an old television set. He graduated from Oxford in 1976, and in the next few years worked for a few high-tech companies in England.

3 Around 1980, Berners-Lee was hired for a short period of time at the European Particle Physics Laboratory (CERN) in Geneva, Switzerland. It was there that he created a software program called Enquire that **linked** documents in the laboratory's information system. The purpose of this system was to **store** a vast amount of information that could be accessed in a very short **time span**. This was the basis for the tool he later created and named the World Wide Web.

4 Berners-Lee left CERN to work for another computer company for a few years. When he returned, he found that his Enquire program had been forgotten. He suggested to his employer that Enquire could be expanded with graphics, text, and video to work on a worldwide basis using the Internet, which had been invented in 1989. But CERN was not a company that could develop such a project. So Berners-Lee worked on his own and created the World Wide Web.

5 Many people think that the World Wide Web and the Internet are the same thing, but they **actually** are not. The Internet is like a large bridge that connects millions of computers around the world and makes it possible for them to communicate with each other. There are different ways to send and receive information over the Internet. These include e-mail,

instant messaging, and, of course, the Web. Each of these ways uses a special set of rules that sends information over the bridge of the Internet.

6 The World Wide Web went on the Internet in 1991. In the beginning, it only had 600,000 users, mostly people in the educational field. But after a while, computer users understood the new **medium**. By 2002, it was estimated that some 600 million people worldwide were using the Web.

7 Undoubtedly, Berners-Lee must have **turned down** numerous offers with which he could have made a lot of money. But making money is not his goal. He is an idealist whose main **pursuit** is knowledge. In 1994, Berners-Lee joined the Laboratory for Computer Science at the Massachusetts Institute of Technology (M.I.T.). He has been working there quietly since, and his earnings as director are probably no more than $90,000 a year. He keeps a **low profile** and can walk the streets of his city unrecognized. He can devote time to his wife and two children.

8 By 1995, *Internet* and *World Wide Web* were familiar words. These inventions made a huge **impact on** modern business and communication. The Web has become a way for many businesses to sell themselves and their products. Companies started to include Web addresses on their business cards and in their advertising. On computer screens today, there are flashing and moving images and advertising of all kinds.

9 Now, some people think there are things on the Web that are **distasteful**. They want governments to keep this kind of material off of the Web. But Berners-Lee thinks the Web should not be **censored**. He said, "You don't go down the street, after all, picking up every piece of paper blowing in the breeze. If you find that a search engine gives you garbage, don't use it. If you don't like your paper, don't buy it." (*Technology Review*, 1996 July, pp. 32–40)

10 Berners-Lee *is* concerned about security on the Web. He suggests having an on-screen **icon** called, "Oh, Yeah?" that can be used by someone who is unsure about something they see on the Web. For example, if someone was shopping online and wanted to make sure that they could trust the company, he or she could click on the icon to receive confirmation that it was safe.

11 Berners-Lee has received numerous awards for his work on the Web, including a knighthood in 2003 by Queen Elizabeth II for services to the global development of the Internet. This now makes him "Sir Timothy

Berners-Lee." Berners-Lee has fought hard to keep the World Wide Web open with no ownership, so it is free for all of us to use. We do not know how Berners-Lee will shape the future of the Web. He hopes the Web will become a tool for social change and wants to be a part of that development. The World Wide Web has already revolutionized the way the world learns; now Berners-Lee hopes it can make the world a better place to live.

VOCABULARY

MEANING

Circle the letter of the answer that is closest in meaning to the underlined word.

1. The purpose of this system was to <u>store</u> a vast amount of information.
   a. use
   b. create
   c. put together
   d. keep

2. After a while, computer users understood the new <u>medium</u>.
   a. machine used to send information
   b. way of communicating
   c. subject to study
   d. knowledge to complete a task

3. Berners-Lee thinks the Web should not be <u>censored</u>.
   a. examined for removal
   b. added to
   c. changed
   d. sold

4. Berners-Lee is a quiet man who does not like the <u>spotlight</u>.
   a. loud noise
   b. crowded areas
   c. a lot of attention
   d. lots of money

5. Some people think there are things on the Web that are <u>distasteful</u>.
   a. likeable
   b. complicated
   c. unpleasant
   d. incorrect

6. Berners-Lee created a software program called Enquire that <u>linked</u> documents.
   a. separated
   b. connected
   c. discovered
   d. saved

7. He is an idealist whose main <u>pursuit</u> is knowledge.
   a. effort
   b. problem
   c. fear
   d. idea

8. He is not <u>outrageously</u> rich or famous.
   a. outwardly
   b. unkindly
   c. understandably
   d. shockingly

9. Many people think that the World Wide Web and the Internet are the same thing, but they <u>actually</u> are not.
   a. unbelievably
   b. almost
   c. usually
   d. truly

10. He suggests having an on-screen <u>icon</u> called, "Oh, Yeah?"
    a. word
    b. picture
    c. program
    d. key

WORDS THAT GO TOGETHER

A. Find words in the reading that go together with the words below to make phrases.

1. impact _____
2. _____ messaging
3. contribution _____
4. _____ span
5. turned _____
6. _____ profile
7. _____ name

B. Complete the sentences with the phrases from Part A.

1. If you _____ something, you refused it.
2. _____ is a very fast way to communicate with someone over the Internet.
3. If someone is famous and everybody knows about him or her, then he or she is a _____.
4. If an object, idea, situation, or person has an effect on others, it has an _____ them.
5. A length of time over which something continues is a _____.
6. If you avoid drawing attention to yourself and your actions, you are keeping a _____.
7. If you are doing something to help others, you are making a _____ them or their cause.

C. Now use the phrases in your own sentences.

Example: *I turned down* the job offer because it didn't pay enough money.

USE

Work with a partner to answer the questions. Use complete sentences.

1. What are three important inventions of the twentieth century that had an *impact on* people's lives?
2. Who is *outrageously* rich or famous in your country?
3. What is *censored* in your country?
4. What kind of behavior do you find *distasteful*?

5. What person has made an important *contribution to* your happiness?
6. Who in your country is a *household name*?
7. What would you do if you had to keep a *low profile*?
8. Where in your home can you *store* things?

COMPREHENSION

UNDERSTANDING MAIN IDEAS

Circle the letter of the best answer.

1. Paragraph 2 is mostly about _____.
   a. where Berners-Lee grew up
   b. the influence of Berners-Lee's parents on his career
   c. Berners-Lee's achievements at Oxford
   d. Berners-Lee's earliest efforts with computers

2. Paragraph 5 is mostly about how the Internet _____.
   a. is like a bridge
   b. works
   c. is different from the Web
   d. uses special rules

3. The main idea of paragraph 8 is that _____.
   a. the *Internet* and *World Wide Web* are familiar words to people
   b. businesses use the Web to sell themselves and their products
   c. the Internet and the World Wide Web have made a big impact on business and communication
   d. companies have started to include Web addresses on their business cards and advertising

4. Paragraph 10 is mainly about how _____.
   a. Berners-Lee wants to have an on-screen icon called "Oh, Yeah?"
   b. Berners-Lee wants to improve security on the Web
   c. an online shopper might not trust a company
   d. people can't shop safely on the Web

REMEMBERING DETAILS

Reread the passage and answer the questions. Write complete sentences.

1. How many users did the World Wide Web have at the beginning, and who were they?

   _____

2. What kind of work did Berners-Lee's parents do?

   _____

3. What has Berners-Lee fought hard to do?

   _____

4. What do some people want governments to do on the Web?

   _____

5. What did the Enquire program do?

   _____

6. What are three different ways to transport information over the Internet?

   _____

7. Why did Queen Elizabeth II give Berners-Lee a knighthood?

   _____

8. What does the World Wide Web permit computer users to do?

   _____

MAKING INFERENCES

The answers to these questions can be inferred, or guessed, from the reading. Circle the letter of the best answer.

1. The reading implies that _____.
   a. Berners-Lee would like more people to acknowledge his great invention
   b. the World Wide Web is not as important as many people say it is
   c. the World Wide Web can be compared to the greatest inventions in history
   d. the World Wide Web had only a small effect on the Internet

2. From the reading, you can conclude that _____.
   a. Berners-Lee's parents were a bad influence on him
   b. Berners-Lee grew up poor
   c. Berners-Lee's childhood had a lot to do with his success
   d. Berners-Lee knew nothing about computers until he graduated from Oxford

3. From the reading, you can conclude that the World Wide Web was _____.

   a. not an immediate success
   b. a big success right after it was invented
   c. a disappointment to many people
   d. only for people in the field of computer science

4. From the reading, it can be concluded that Berners-Lee _____.
   a. knew from the beginning that his Enquire program would be used worldwide
   b. believes that work and family are more important than fame and fortune
   c. wishes he had never invented the World Wide Web
   d. thinks he has not received the money he deserves for his invention

5. The reading implies that Berners-Lee _____.
   a. is not interested in the future of the World Wide Web
   b. thinks people should continue using the Web even if they don't like it
   c. would like to see all harmful information taken off the Web
   d. wants his invention to be good for society

DISCUSSION

Discuss the answers to these questions with your classmates.

1. What are the positive and negative aspects of the World Wide Web?
2. How can the World Wide Web be used as a tool for social change? Is social change always a good thing? Why or why not?
3. How has the World Wide Web made the world a better place?
4. Should Berners-Lee have accepted fame and fortune? What is your opinion of the choices he has made in his life?

WRITING

On separate paper, write a paragraph or an essay about one of the following topics:

1. What are the advantages and / or disadvantages of using the Internet or the World Wide Web?

2. Should the World Wide Web be censored? Give reasons.

3. How has the World Wide Web changed the way people buy things?

GRAMMAR AND PUNCTUATION

 THE DEFINITE ARTICLE: INVENTIONS AND THE MEDIA

1. Usually, *the* is not used with nouns that represent a general group or the idea of something. However, *the* <u>is</u> used when referring to an invention in general.

   He works with computers. <u>but</u> *He invented **the** computer.*

2. *The* has special uses in references to the media (ways of communicating). For example, when referring to the radio and television media, we say:

   *I listen to **the** radio a lot.* <u>but</u> *I watch a lot of television.*

   However, we do use *the* when talking about an actual television set.

   *I turned off **the** television and went to work.*

Fill in the blanks with *the* or *X* for no definite article.

1. _____ printing press is one of the world's most important inventions.

2. He put _____ television in his bedroom.

3. _____ computer has changed our lives.

4. When he was a child, his parents often talked about _____ computers.

5. _____ instant message may be the fastest way to communicate today.

6. The twentieth century brought amazing investions in _____ technology.

7. Before _____ television, we had _____ radio.

8. _____ society is better today because of the Internet.

9. When was _____ computer invented?

10. Do you prefer to play computer games or to watch _____ television?

SELF-TEST 2
Units 9–16

A. SENTENCE COMPLETION

Circle the letter of the correct answer.

1. CyberAngels is _____ the Web safer for us to use.
   - a. an organization that makes
   - b. organization that makes
   - c. a organization that makes
   - d. an organization that make

2. Many people _____ to climb Everest, but none were successful until 1953.
   - a. are tried
   - b. had tried
   - c. have tried
   - d. try

3. _____ Renaissance as the beginning of modern history.
   - a. Some people think that the
   - b. Some people think of the
   - c. Some people think about the
   - d. Any people think of the

4. Football has _____ players than any other sport.
   - a. the most
   - b. many
   - c. more
   - d. as much

5. Convicts _____ western Australia, but around 1850, the colony there asked for them.
   - a. have never been sent to
   - b. had ever been sent to
   - c. had never been sent to
   - d. never sent to

6. European greetings _____.
   - a. variety from shaking to kissing
   - b. varies from shaking hands to kissing
   - c. vary from shaking hands to kiss
   - d. vary from shaking hands to kissing

7. Napoleon was _____ army commander.
    a. an outstanding as   c. outstanding as a
    b. outstanding as an   d. outstanding

8. Tim Berners-Lee is _____ invented the World Wide Web.
    a. : the man who   c. , the man who
    b. the man who   d. the man; who

B. VOCABULARY

Complete the sentences. Circle the letter of the correct answer.

1. The Guardian Angels took back neighborhoods _____ crime.
    a. pleased with   c. restricted to
    b. infested with   d. betrayed by

2. Today, Mount Everest has lost the _____ it once had.
    a. priority   c. severity
    b. task   d. appeal

3. During the Renaissance, the arts _____.
    a. encouraged   c. collapsed
    b. flourished   d. dared

4. Up to 1999, the World Cup was held _____ in Europe and the
    Americas, but since then it has been held in Asian countries as well.
    a. eventually   c. actually
    b. appropriately   d. alternately

5. Conditions on the first ships transporting convicts to Australia were
    _____.
    a. deplorable   c. distasteful
    b. humiliated   d. unprecedented

6. The usual American greeting is a handshake with a _____.
    a. firm grip   c. physical condition
    b. down payment   d. time span

7. Napoleon was _____ power.
   a. pleased with   c. known as
   b. assigned to   d. driven by

8. We don't hear much about the man who invented the Web because he doesn't like the _____ .
   a. pursuit   c. summit
   b. spotlight   d. medium

C. GRAMMAR AND PUNCTUATION

Circle the letter of the sentence or sentences with the correct grammar and punctuation.

1. a. Guardian Angels is a volunteer organization that protects the people from the criminals.
   b. Guardian Angels is volunteer organization that protects people from criminals.
   c. Guardian Angels is a volunteer organization that protects people from the criminals.
   d. Guardian Angels is a volunteer organization that protects people from criminals.

2. a. Mount Everest is in the Himalayas, a mountain range in the India, the Nepal, and the Tibet.
   b. Mount Everest is in the Himalayas, a mountain range in India, Nepal, and Tibet.
   c. The Mount Everest is in Himalayas, a mountain range in the India, Nepal, and Tibet.
   d. Mount Everest is in Himalayas, a mountain range in India, Nepal, and Tibet.

3. a. The art of the Renaissance began in Florence although it spread to other cities.
   b. Although the art of the Renaissance spread to other cities, it began in Florence.
   c. The art of the Renaissance spread to other cities though it began in Florence.
   d. The art of the Renaissance spread to other cities. It began in Florence, although.

4. a. Football is the most popular sport in world.
   b. Football is most popular sport in world.
   c. Football is the most popular sport in the world.
   d. Football is most popular sport in the world.

5. a. The British government has shipped convicts to America until the settlement in New South Wales was established.
   b. The British government shipped convicts to America until the settlement in New South Wales is established.
   c. The British government had shipped convicts to America until the settlement in New South Wales was established.
   d. The British government had shipping convicts to America until the settlement in New South Wales was established.

6. a. In some countries, the greeting is a kiss. In other, it is a handshake.
   b. In some countries, the greeting is a kiss. In another, it is a handshake.
   c. In some countries, the greeting is a kiss. In the other, it is a handshake.
   d. In some countries, the greeting is a kiss. In others, it is a handshake.

7. a. After the revolution, Napoleon ruled wise and well and restored law and order.
   b. After the revolution, Napoleon ruled wisely and well and restored law and ordering.
   c. After the revolution, Napoleon ruled wisely and well and restoring law and orderly.
   d. After the revolution, Napoleon ruled wisely and well and restored law and order.

8. a. Tim Berners-Lee invented the World Wide Web, but not the computer.
   b. Tim Berners-Lee invented World Wide Web, but not computers.
   c. Tim Berners-Lee invented the World Wide Web, but not radio.
   d. Tim Berners-Lee invented World Wide Web, but not television.

APPENDICES

WORD LIST

UNIT 1

Vocabulary

		Words that Go Together	
conflict	precious	combination of	made predictions
encounter	prosperity	good deeds	passed down from
exotic	site	in trouble	throughout history
inspired	theories	known as	
mist	universal		

UNIT 2

Vocabulary

		Words that Go Together	
abandoned	frail	at intervals	serving in the
allowed	knots	in exchange for	army
claimed	neglect	majority of	stood for
collapsed	sophisticated	on special occasions	under control
eligible	starved		

UNIT 3

Vocabulary

		Words that Go Together	
colleagues	shrine	depending upon	rows of
displays	significance	let . . . know	short for
formal	spotless	make sure that	take part in
harmony	thoroughly	pay . . . a visit	
honored	triumphs		

UNIT 4

Vocabulary

		Words that Go Together	
astonished	granted	carried out	spin a tale
betrayed	implored	devoted to	went out of his
dazzled	rejoiced	do a service for	mind
depict	reluctance	lost her senses	
executed	unfaithful	put off	

UNIT 5

Vocabulary

		Words that Go Together	
abolished	inferior	basis of	material things
brow	loyalty	code of ethics	noble spirit
esteem	privileges	influence of	once again
frugal	rebels	martial arts	
industrialized	status		

UNIT 6

Vocabulary

demonstrate	layers
fake	reflect
flattered	reveal
imitated	ridicule
intimidate	sensuous

Words that Go Together

a symbol of	make a fashion
in mourning	statement
in public	marital status
limited to	save time

UNIT 7

Vocabulary

disposable	fuel
durable	hometown
eliminate	odor
eventually	unique
forever	variations

Words that Go Together

according to	left behind
found the solution	react to
heat resistant	thrown out
in honor of	

UNIT 8

Vocabulary

adopted	fidelity
available	indicate
considering	piled
eternity	switch
fertility	vein

Words that Go Together

associated with	down payment
be aware of	in common
common practice	vice versa
did not matter	

UNIT 9

Vocabulary

attitude	hire
deteriorated	muggers
dismissed	online
escort	resources
fraud	transit

Words that Go Together

at all	ride the subway
checking your e-mail	sneak into
infested with	volunteer
law enforcement	organization

UNIT 10

Vocabulary

appeal	novelty
attempt	prestige
challenging	risk
dared	summit
mystique	unprecedented

Words that Go Together

fascination with	physical
go ahead with	condition
in advance	pleased with
inner strength	waiting their turn

UNIT 11

Vocabulary

affected	flourished
blended	marks
conventions	obstacles
encouraged	preserve
era	stage

Words that Go Together

as a result of	setting out
brought . . . about	way of life
in the direction of	works of art
passion for	

UNIT 12

Vocabulary

alternately	devised
appropriately	entirely
banned	promote
besides	surpasses
counterparts	trend

Words that Go Together

concentrate on	sporting event
ever since	started out
public property	team sports
school curriculum	

UNIT 13

Vocabulary

acknowledge	labor
condemned	policy
convicts	predecessor
deplorable	severity
grateful	task

Words that Go Together

assigned to	served out their
breaking the law	sentences
made it	set free
on board	
safe and sound	

UNIT 14

Vocabulary

applaud	offended
averted	palms
bow	priority
embrace	sniffing
insight	

Words that Go Together

business transaction	opt for
firm grip	restricted to
flick of the eyebrows	supposed to
nod their heads	the norm

UNIT 15

Vocabulary

bitter	fields
conquered	foundation
declared	humiliated
defeating	pose
dignified	wisdom

Words that Go Together

driven by	perform the
had no choice but to	ceremony
law and order	went to war with
lose control	won a victory

UNIT 16

Vocabulary

actually	medium
censored	outrageously
distasteful	pursuit
icon	spotlight
linked	store

Words that Go Together

contribution to	low profile
household name	time span
impact on	turned down
instant messaging	

MAP OF THE WORLD

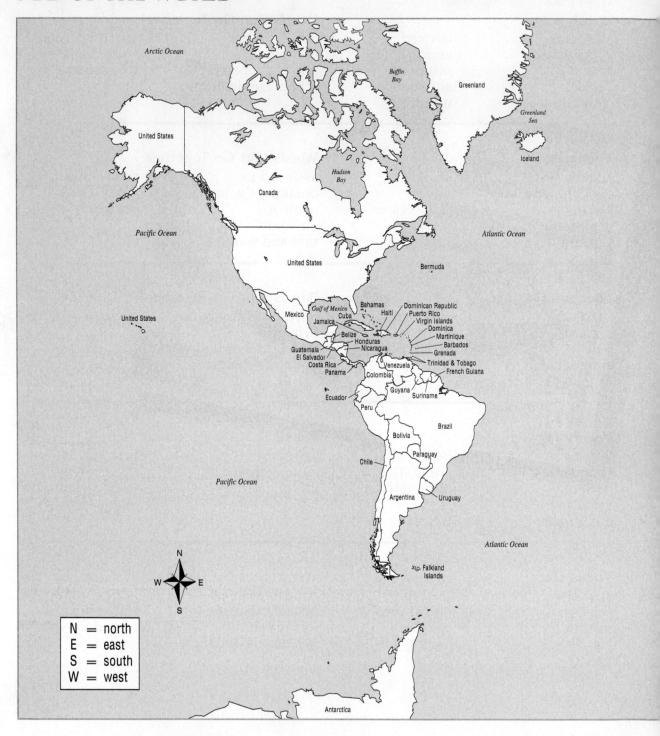

Arctic Ocean

Baffin Bay

Greenland

Greenland Sea

Iceland

United States

Canada

Hudson Bay

Pacific Ocean

Atlantic Ocean

United States

Bermuda

United States

Mexico

Gulf of Mexico

Bahamas

Cuba

Jamaica

Belize

Honduras

Guatemala

El Salvador

Nicaragua

Costa Rica

Panama

Dominican Republic

Puerto Rico

Haiti

Virgin Islands

Dominica

Martinique

Barbados

Grenada

Trinidad & Tobago

French Guiana

Venezuela

Colombia

Guyana

Suriname

Ecuador

Peru

Brazil

Bolivia

Paraguay

Chile

Argentina

Uruguay

Pacific Ocean

Atlantic Ocean

Falkland Islands

N

W E

S

Antarctica

N = north
E = east
S = south
W = west

Arctic Ocean

Arctic Ocean

Barents Sea

Bering Sea

Sweden

Russia

Finland

Norway

Britain   *North Sea*   Azerbaijan   Kazakhstan   Mongolia   North Korea   *Sea of Japan*

Ireland   Uzbekistan   Japan

France   Georgia   Kyrgystan   China   South Korea   *East China Sea*   Pacific Ocean

Black Sea   Tajikistan

Portugal   Spain   Turkey   Armenia   Turkmenistan   Afghanistan   Burma (Myanmar)   Taiwan   Hong Kong

Caspian Sea

Mediterranean Sea   Cyprus   Syria   Iraq   Kuwait   Iran   Nepal   Bhutan   Laos

Morocco   Tunisia   Lebanon   Jordan   Bahrain   Qatar   Pakistan   Bangladesh   Vietnam

Western Sahara   Algeria   Libya   Israel   Egypt   Saudi Arabia   United Arab Emirates   India   Thailand   *South China Sea*   Cambodia   Brunei   Guam/Marianas

Senegal   Mauritania   Mali   Niger   Chad   Sudan   Yemen   *Arabian Sea*   Sri Lanka   Singapore   Malaysia   Philippines   Marshall Islands

Gambia   Benin   Eritrea   Djibouti   Micronesia   Papua New Guinea   Solomon Islands

Guinea Bissau   Guinea   Nigeria   Central African Republic   Ethiopia   Somalia   Indonesia   E. Timor

Sierra Leone   Liberia   Cameroon   Uganda   Rwanda   Kenya   Coral Sea   Fiji

Côte D'ivoire   Ghana   Togo   Burkina Faso   Equitorial Guinea   Gabon   Congo   Zaire   Tanzania   Malawi   Indian Ocean   Australia

Angola   Zambia   Mauritius   New Zealand

Namibia   Botswana   Madagascar

Zimbabwe   Mozambique

South Africa   Swaziland   Lesotho

Atlantic Ocean

Antarctica

Norway   *Baltic Sea*   Estonia   Russia

Denmark   Sweden   Latvia

Netherlands   Russia   Lithuania

Belgium   Poland   Belarus

Germany   Ukraine

Luxembourg   Czech Republic   Slovakia   Yugoslavia (Serbia-Montenegro)   Moldova

France   Switzerland   Austria   Hungary   Romania

Slovenia   Croatia   *Black Sea*

Italy   Bulgaria

Bosnia Herzegovenia   Macedonia   Turkey

Albania   Greece

INDEX TO THE GRAMMAR AND PUNCTUATION ACTIVITIES

UNIT	GRAMMAR AND PUNCTUATION	PAGE
1 What Is the Legend of King Arthur?	Subject-Verb Agreement	10
2 Why Did the Inca Empire Disappear?	Commas: With Transitional Expressions— *However, For Example, Therefore, As a Matter of Fact*	20
3 How Do Hindus Celebrate the Diwali Festival?	Direct and Indirect Speech	30
4 What Is the Story Behind *The 1,001 Arabian Nights*?	Participial Adjectives	41
5 Who Were the Samurai?	Semicolons	51
6 What Does Hair Tell Us About People?	Commas: After Introductory Words and Phrases	61
7 How Did Chopsticks Originate?	Hyphens	70
8 Where Did Certain Wedding Customs Come From?	Commas: To Separate Interrupters	80
9 Who Are the CyberAngels?	Articles: *A, An, The*	95
10 Why Do People Want to Climb Mount Everest?	The Definite Article: Geographical Names and Directions	106
11 Why Is the Renaissance Important?	Showing Contrast: *Though, Although; Despite, In Spite Of*	118
12 What Is the Most Popular Sport in the World?	The Definite Article: Nationalities and Unique Nouns	128
13 How Did Convicts Help Settle Australia?	The Past Perfect	139
14 How Do Greetings Differ Around the World?	Forms of *Other*	150
15 Why Is Napoleon Famous?	Parallel Structure	161
16 Who Invented the World Wide Web?	The Definite Article: Inventions and the Media	172